Preserving Dundas

Building memories one picture at a time

Written and photographed by Barbara A. Fanson

Published by Sterling Education Centre Inc.

Thank you for reading.
If you have a moment, please post a review on Amazon.

For other books by the same author:
http://fanson.net

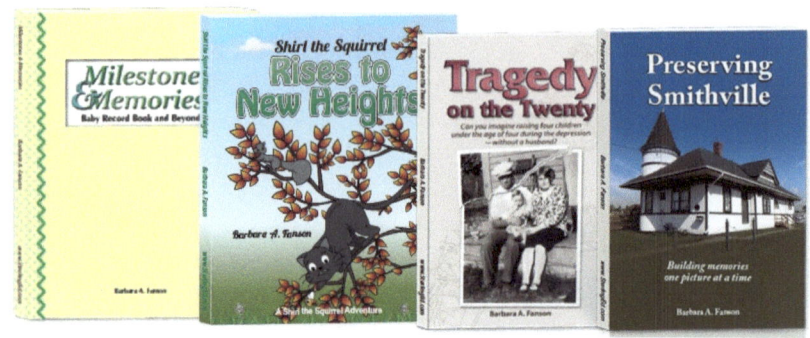

Other books by Barbara Fanson:

Preserving Smithville, building memories one picture at a time, published by Sterling Education Centre.

Tragedy on the Twenty, a historical fiction about an accident on Hwy. 20 in 1933 published by Sterling Education Centre.

Milestones & Memories, a baby record book and beyond, published by Sterling Education Centre.

Shirl the Squirrel Rises to New Heights, a children's picture book published by Sterling Education Centre.

Start & Run a Desktop Publishing Business, published by Self-Counsel Press.

Preserving Dundas
Building memories one picture at a time

Copyright © 2018 Barbara A. Fanson
All Rights Reserved. Most photos taken in September 2018.
Book ISBN: 978-1-989361-01-6
Electronic Book ISBN: 978-1-989361-00-9
No part of this publication may be reproduced or stored in a retrieval system, or transmitted in any form or by any means, electronic, mechanical, recording, or otherwise, without written permission of the publisher:
Sterling Education Centre Inc.
220 Homebrook Drive, Mount Hope, ON L0R 1W0
Email: learn@sterlinged.com   Phone: (905) 679-9229

Dundas Walking Tour

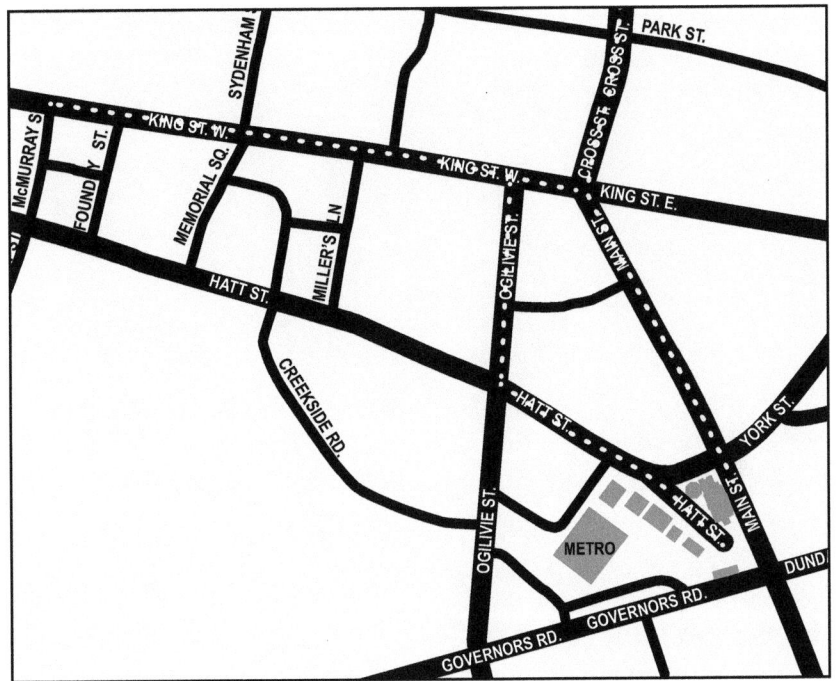

You can start anywhere along this route.

Dundas Walking Tour Map 3

Dundas, Ontario: Valley Town 5

Main Street 7

Cross Street 19

King Street 30

Ogilvie Street 55

Hatt Street 57

Barbara A. Fanson

Edwardian-style house

Brackets
(or dentil blocks)

Gable
(with scalloped shingles)

Cornice Return

Doric Column

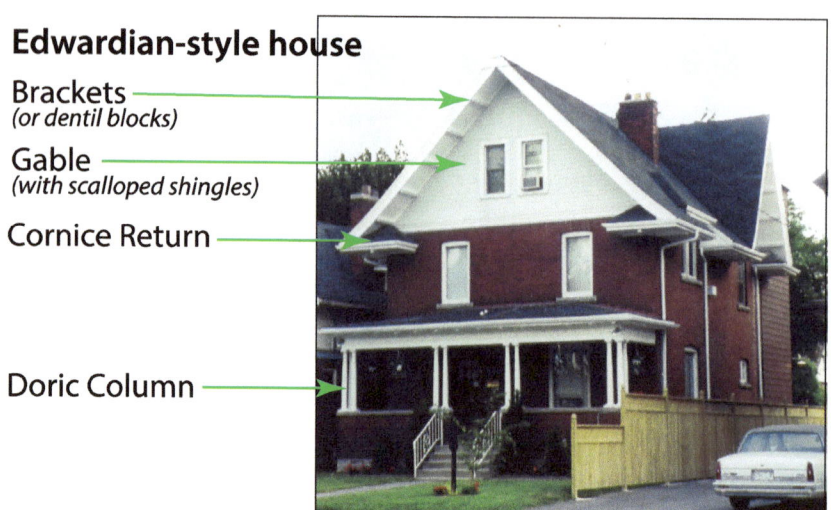

In 1997, I renovated this Edwardian-style house with large gables and scalloped shingles, dentil blocks or brackets under the roof, and cornice returns. The 10 Doric columns, took 9 hours to strip, sand, and repaint each one.

The house was built in 1913.

—Author Barbara A. Fanson

This book is dedicated to all the people
who have painted, renovated, and maintained
their homes.

Thank you for sharing your house with us.

Dundas, Ontario
Valley Town

Dundas, Ontario is famous for having the shortest highway in North America, but the longest running hotel in Ontario, the Collins Hotel.

Dundas, Ontario is nestled at the bottom of the Niagara Peninsula on the western end of Lake Ontario, hence the nickname Valley Town.

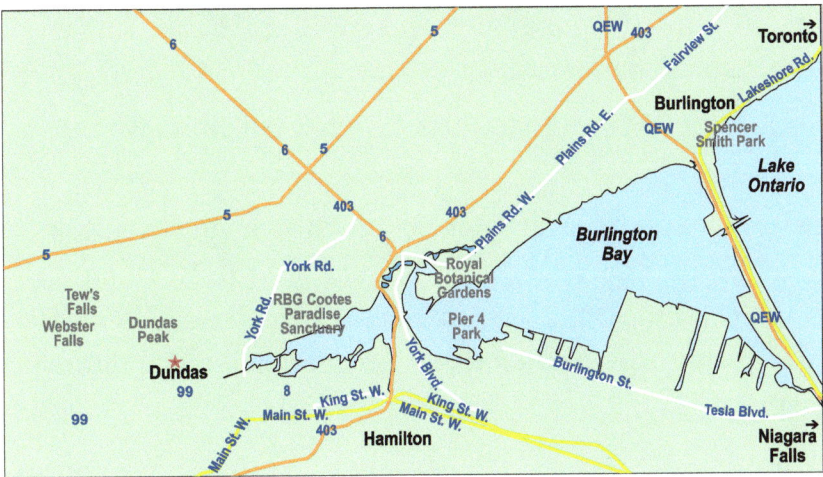

Dundas is located between Burlington and Hamilton in Ontario. A former town, Dundas became part of Hamilton on January 1, 2001 when it amalgamated with the Regional Municipality of Hamilton-Wentworth and its six municipalities: Hamilton, Ancaster, Dundas, Flamborough, Glanbrook, and Stoney Creek.

The town of Dundas was named by John Graves Simcoe, Lieutenant Governor of Upper Canada for his friend Henry Dundas, a Scottish lawyer who has never been to North America. Originally called Coote's Paradise, it was renamed Dundas in 1814.

In 1846 there was six chapels or churches, a fire company and a post office. Industry included two gristmills, a furniture factory, a cloth factory and two foundries (for making steam engines). There were also six taverns, four schools, three breweries and a bank agency operating in Dundas.

The town was incorporated in 1847 and celebrated its sequential—150th birthday—in 1997.

In 1853 the Great Western Railway (GWR) put a railway through Dundas, but it wasn't until 1864 that Dundas got a rail station. By 1869 the population was 3,500 and Dundas had become a small manufacturing centre.

Dundas Street in Toronto leads to Dundas, which is also called Highway 5.

There are two popular festivals held each year: Buskerfest in June and Dundas Cactus Festival in August. In 1976, Dundas became the cactus capital of Canada because the Ben Veldhuis Cactus Greenhouses had achieved international recognition for its Cacti.

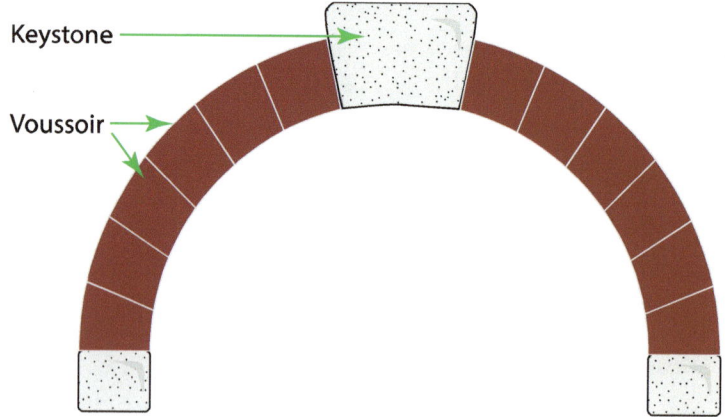

Historical Dundas Walking Tour

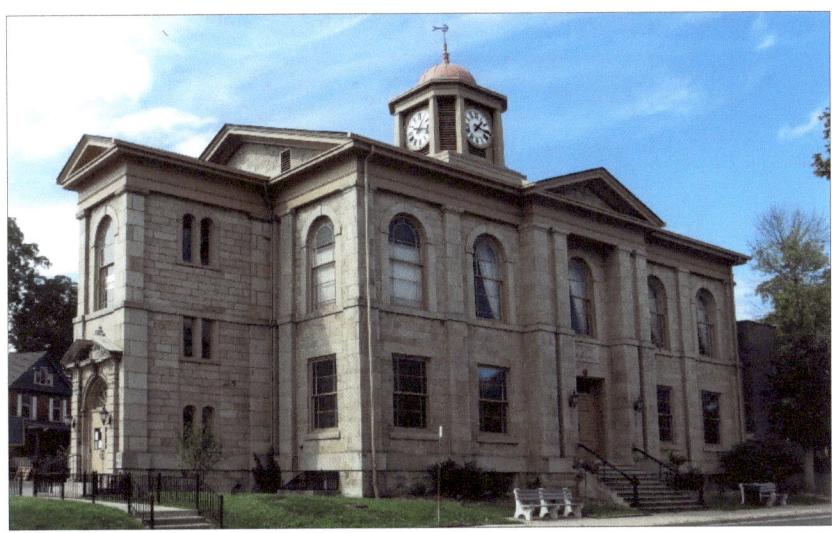

Dundas Town Hall, 60 Main St. was formally opened in 1849. It was built from Whirlpool sandstone, cut as dimension stone. The large lintels (supports across the top of a door or window) and voussoirs are notable.

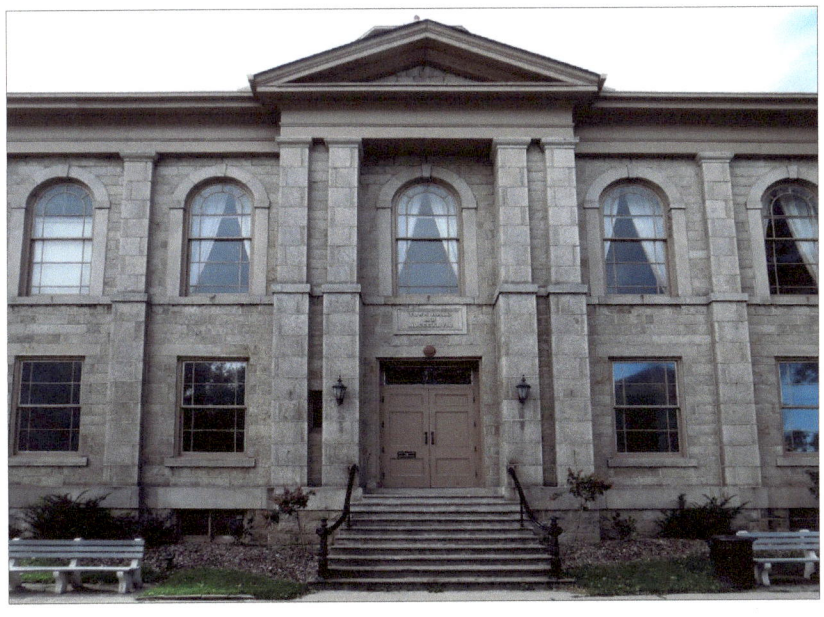

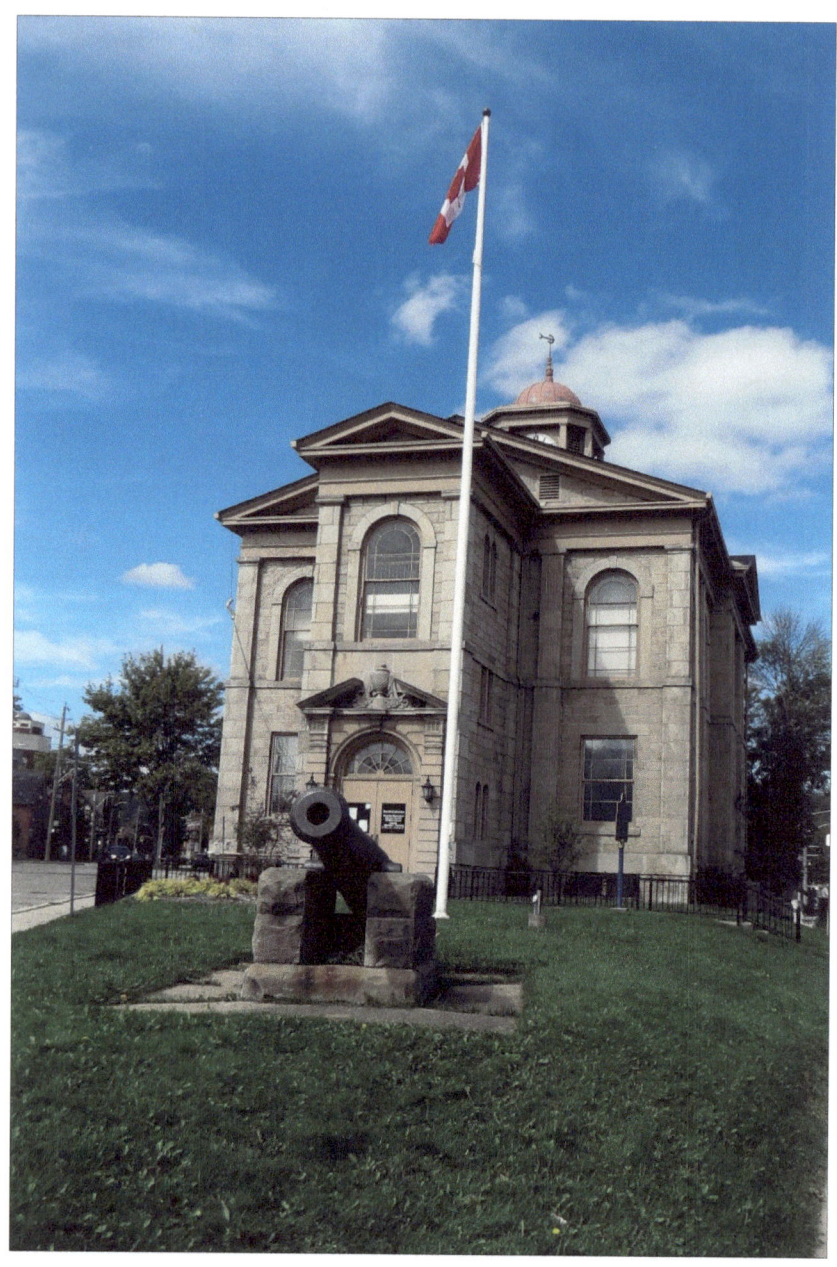

The Dundas Town Hall at 60 Main St. at Hatt St. is one of only five municipal buildings constructed before 1850 remaining in the province with heritage designation.

Dundas was incorporated as a town in 1847 by a special Act of the legislature of the Province of Canada. The following year the town council accepted a tender from a local builder, James Scott, to erect a stone town hall and voted £2000 to cover the cost. Designed in a version of Roman Classic, by Francis Hawkins of Dundas, the building was completed by July 1849, and was said to have cost £2500. Except for a small Italianate wing added later, the exterior has been little altered, although a thorough renovation was carried out in 1946. It is one of the most handsome, pre-1850, municipal buildings surviving in Ontario.

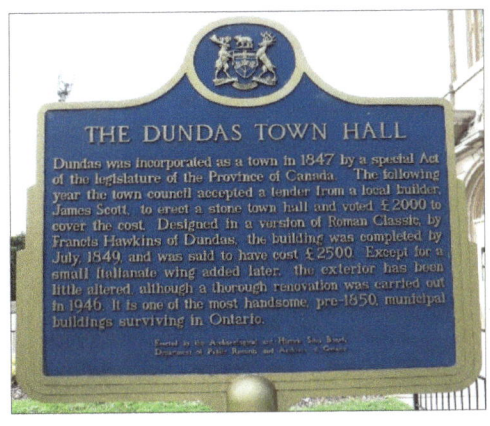

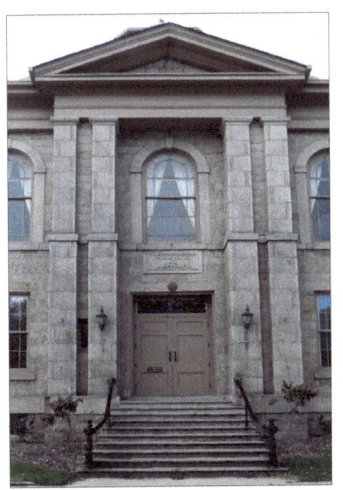

Notice the second story windows have an arch with keystone at the top. The east door has a large pediment above the door supported by large stone columns.

The south—and main door—has an extravagant pediment above the arched door. Notice the corner stones: A.D. 1848.

Barbara A. Fanson

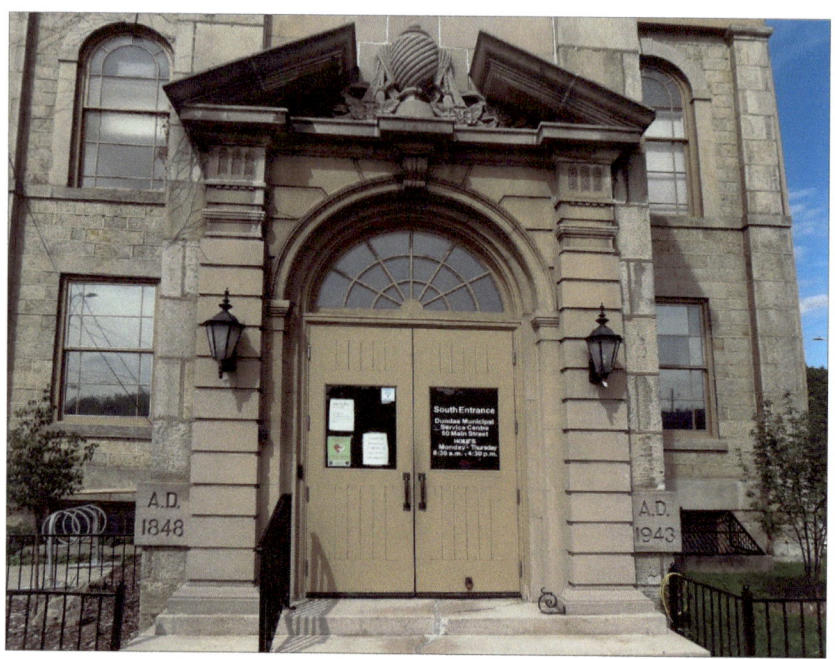

The door on the south side is a late Renaissance style, verging on Baroque. The pediment is broken in many sections with the center being an urn flanked by stylized roses. The keystone features an interesting agraffe. The fanlight is a semi-circular window with a radiating design.

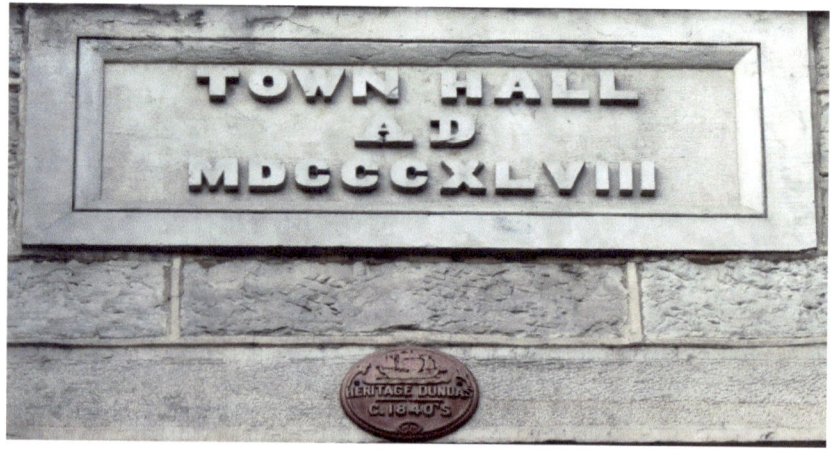

The plaques above the east entrance of Dundas Town Hall.

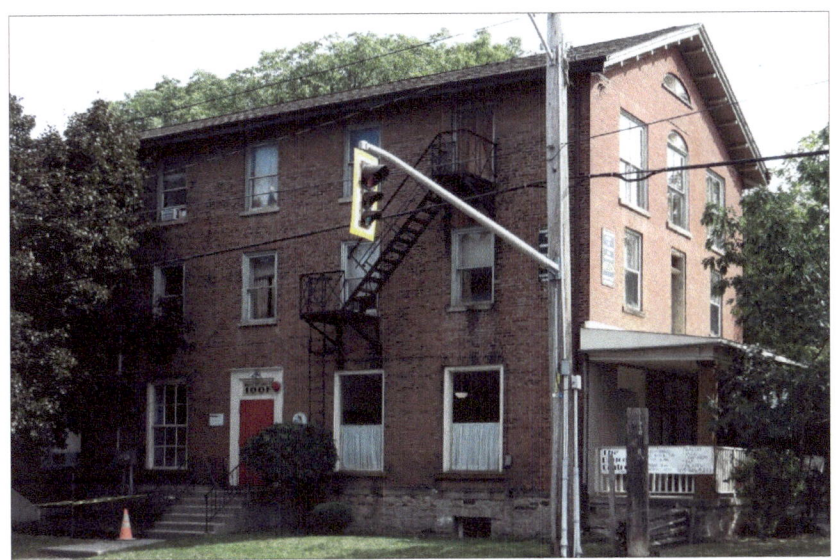

The Valley City Lodge 117 is located at 63 Main St.
The building has a stone basement and large porch.
The Dance Centre practices in the building.

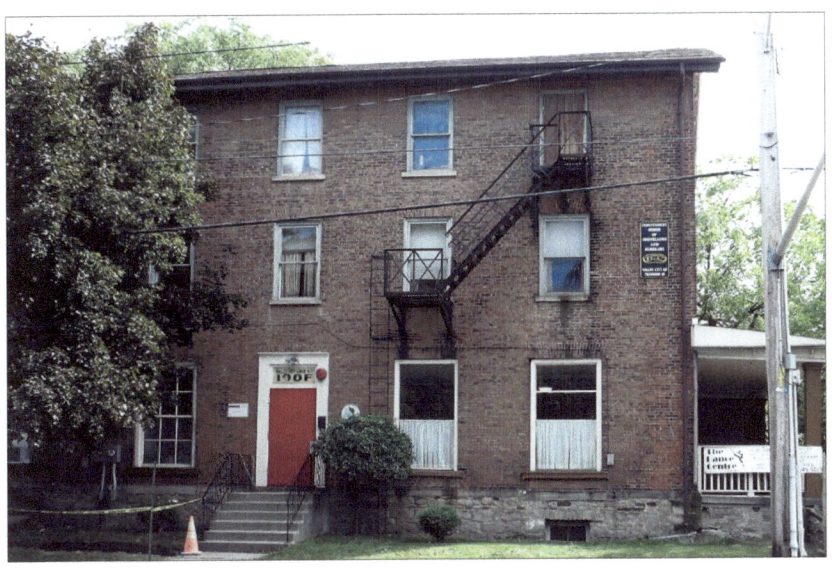

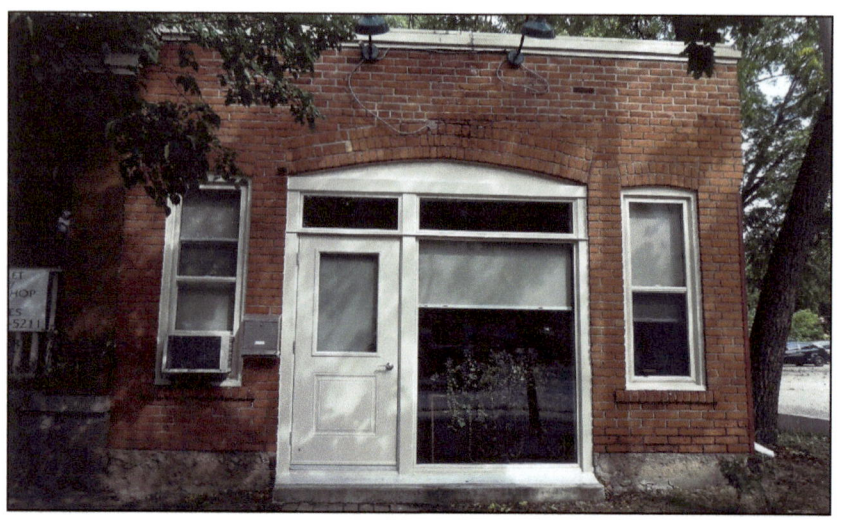

The renovated garage at 63 Main St.

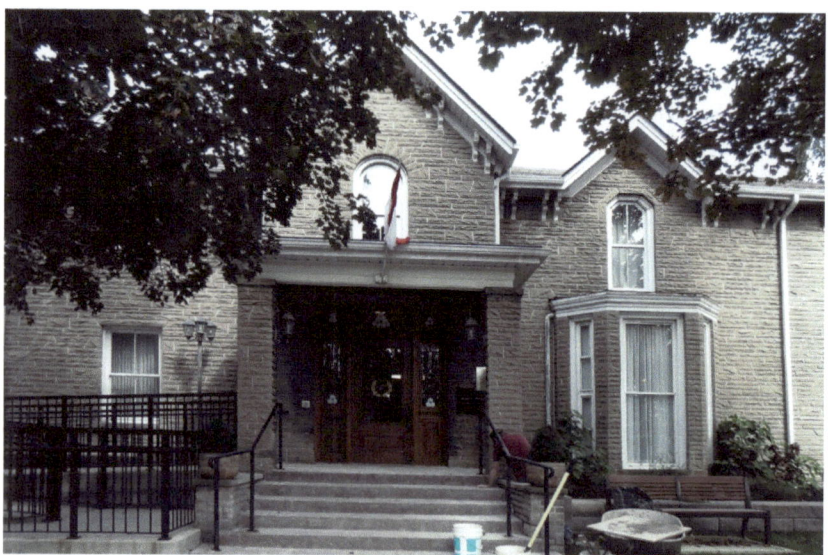

The Turner Family Funeral Home at 53 Main St. is the oldest privately owned funeral home in the Dundas area. The building has a large bay window, a large and two small gables supported by double brackets, and arched windows. Notice the right window on the second floor has bevelled corners. It was purchased by Wallace Cattel in 1939.

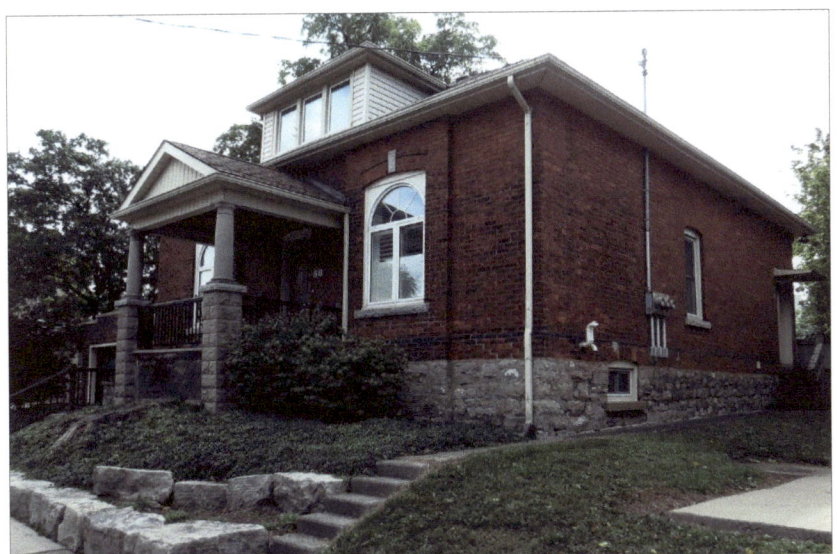

58 Main St. has two stone pillars holding Doric columns supporting the porch roof. Though the windows have been updated, they still have a keystone and arched brickwork.

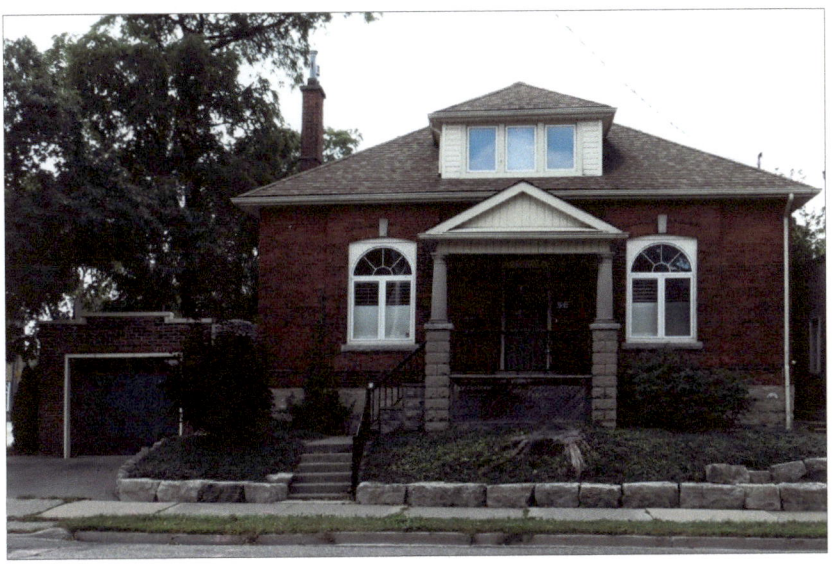

Barbara A. Fanson

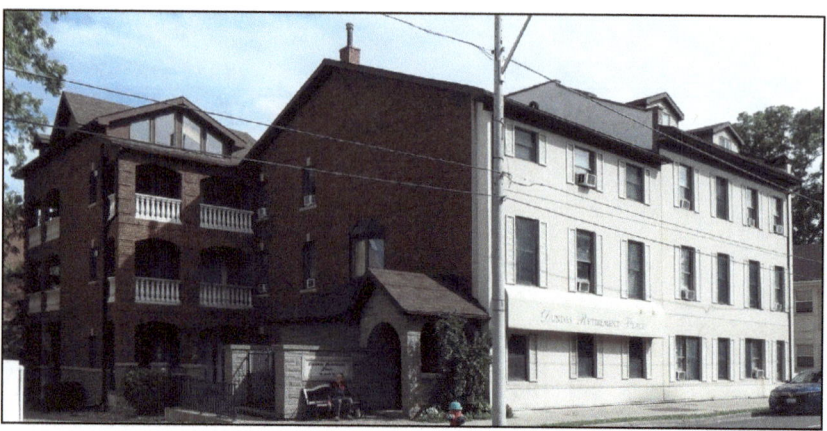

Dundas Retirement Home at 33 Main St. has an older building in the back with two balconies and brick pillars.

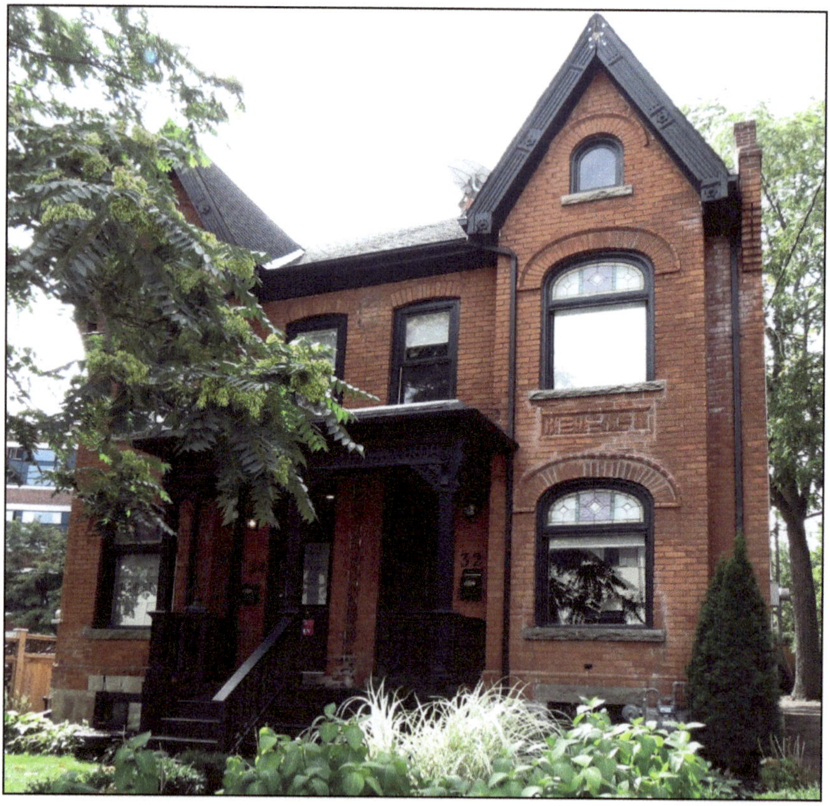

34 and 32 Main St. is a symmetrical duplex with distinctive brick work, arched windows, fancy cornices on the porch.

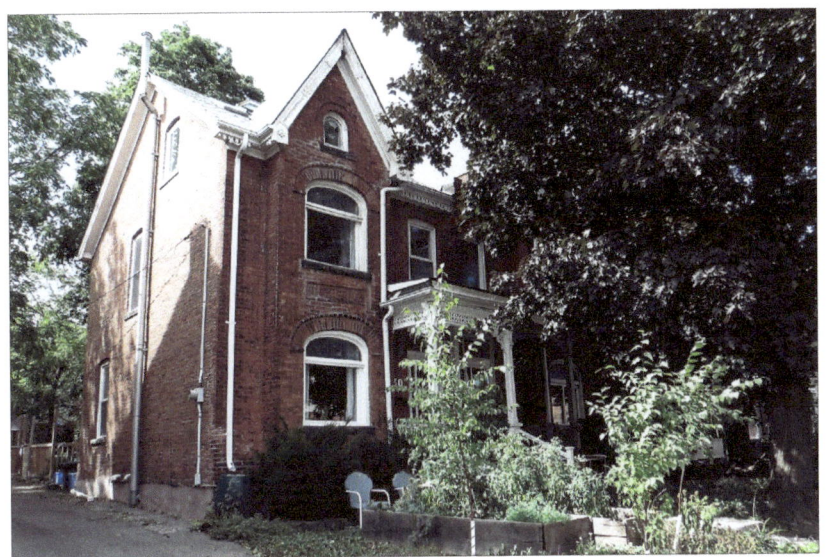

30 and 28 Main Street are similar to the previous duplex, but finished with a white gable and porch.

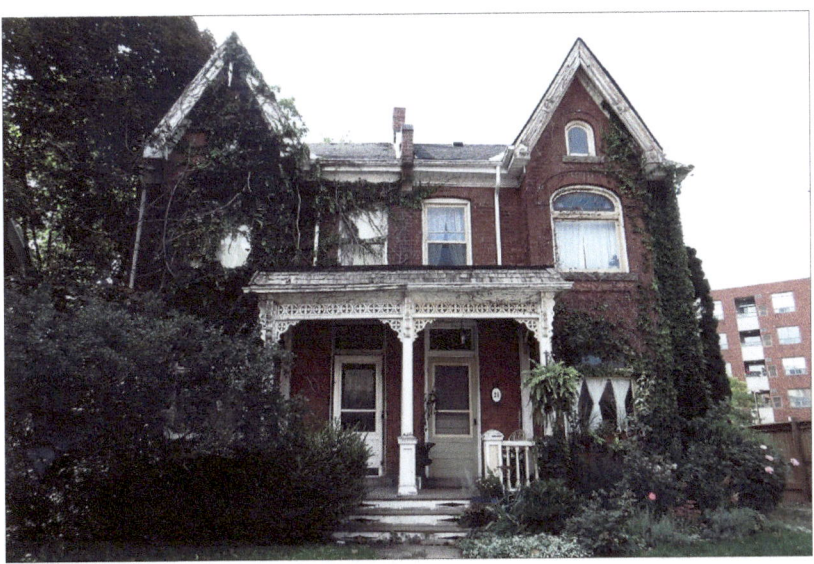

26 and 24 Main Street is another duplex with fancy cornices under the front porch and on the gables. Notice the arched windows.

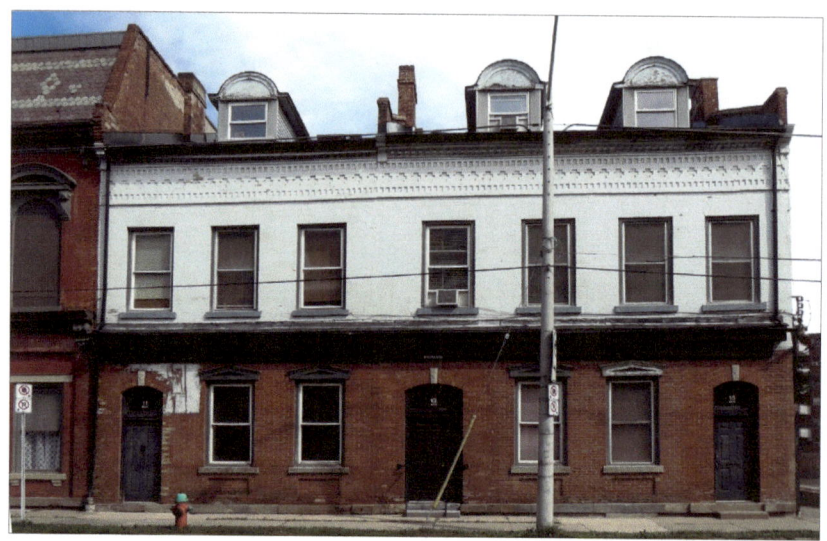

13 Main Street has three dormers on the roof with a rounded roof. The door has an arch and keystone above it. Notice the fancy brick work at the top of the façade.

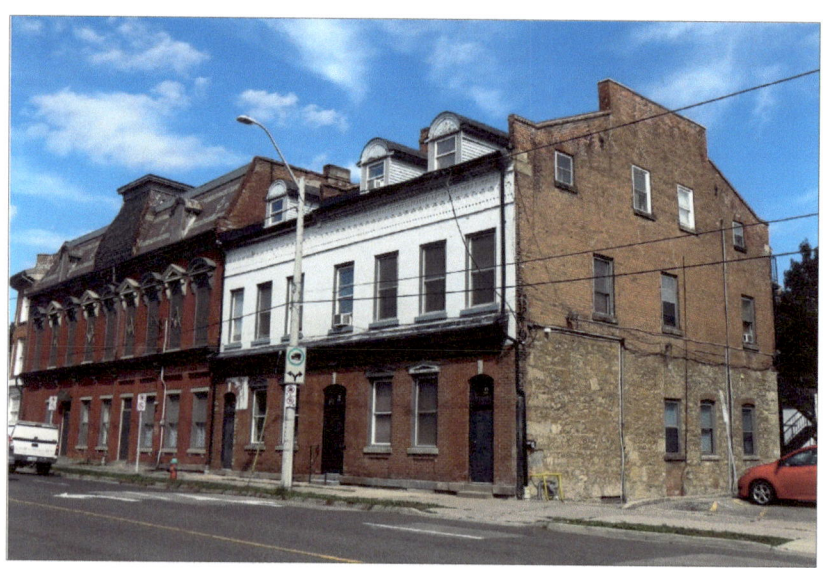

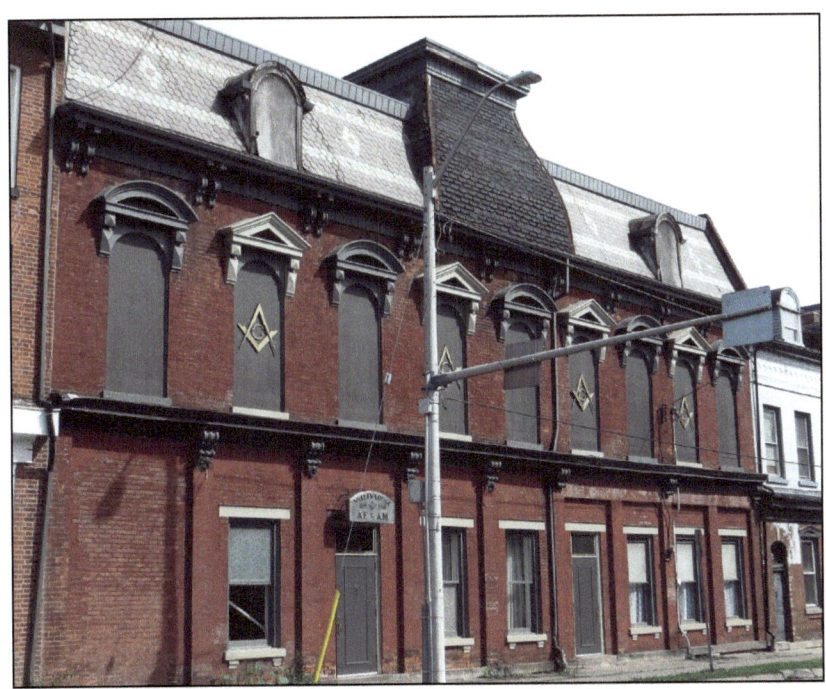

Valley Lodge No. 100 A.F. A.M. on Main Street has two kinds of window hoods above the top windows—some are pointed while some are arched. Notice the pattern in the slate roof. The roof has 2 arched dormers and a massive, unique dormer with shingles.

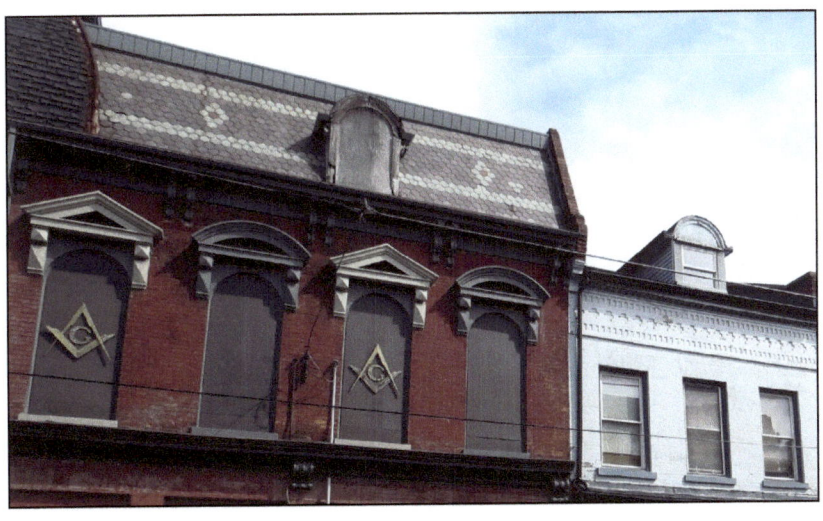

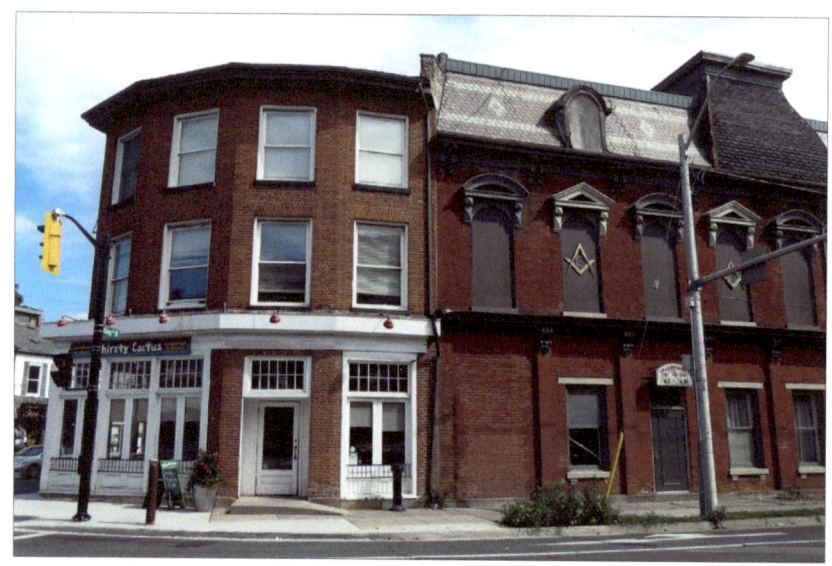

The Thirsty Cactus is a Mexican restaurant at 2 King St. E. The odd-shaped building has unique windows on the ground floor with the smaller window panes panes above.

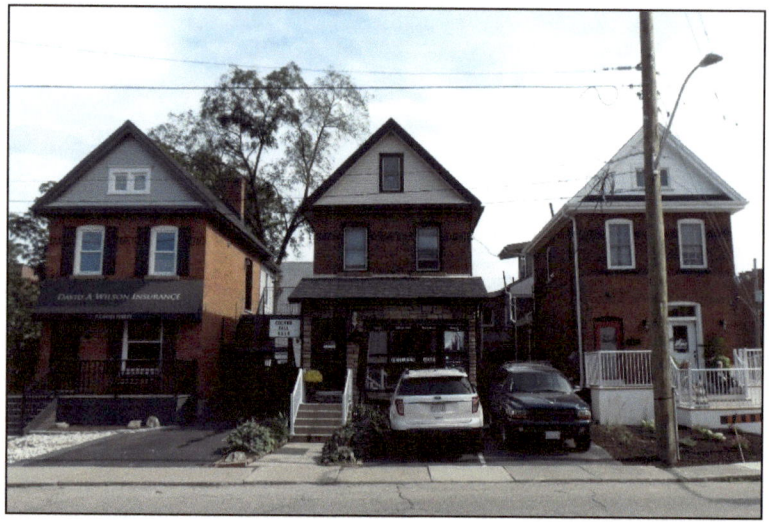

5, 3, and 1 Cross Street have similar features: a gabled roof with window and had a covered porch at one time. David Wilson Insurance, Putrone Salon & Spa, and David William Shoes & more occupy the buildings at this time.

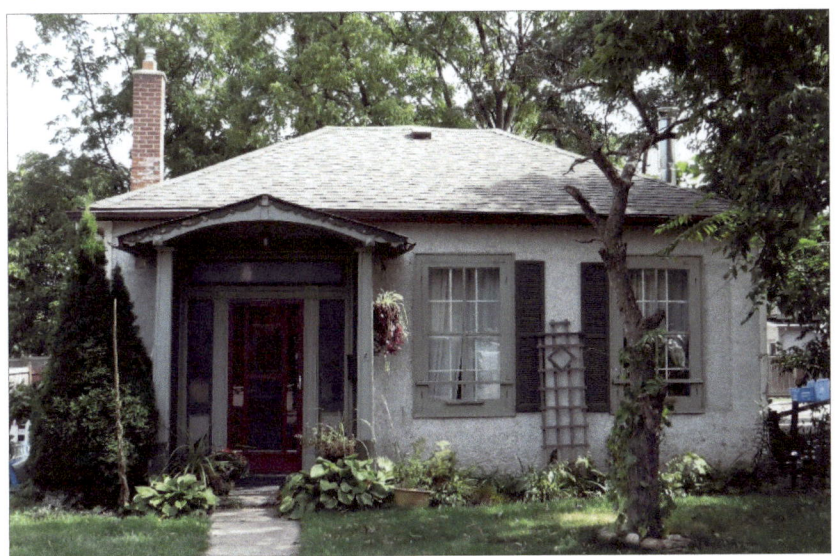

7 Cross Street is a cottage-style house. The slightly-rounded pediment or roof above the entrance is distinctive with windows beside the door. Notice the 12 pane windows.

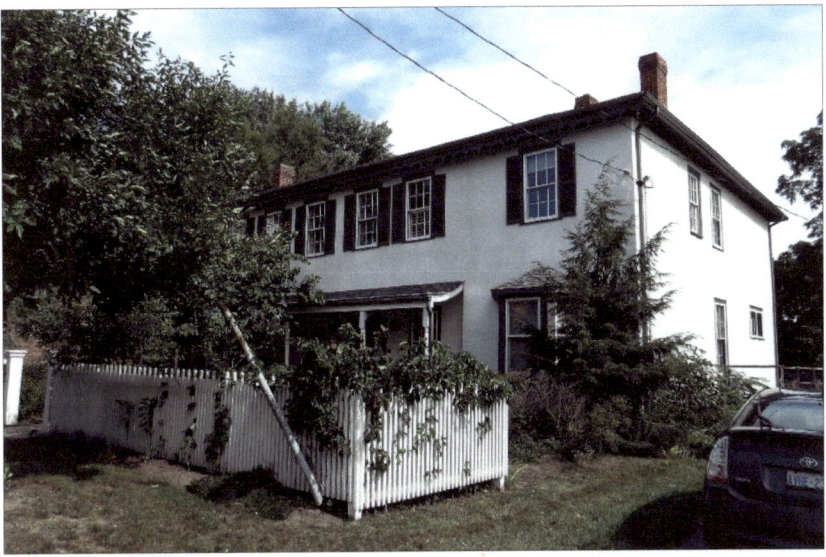

Victoria Hall at 11 Cross Street has a white picket fence and beautiful front porch. The large two story house has several traditional windows with 12 panes of glass.

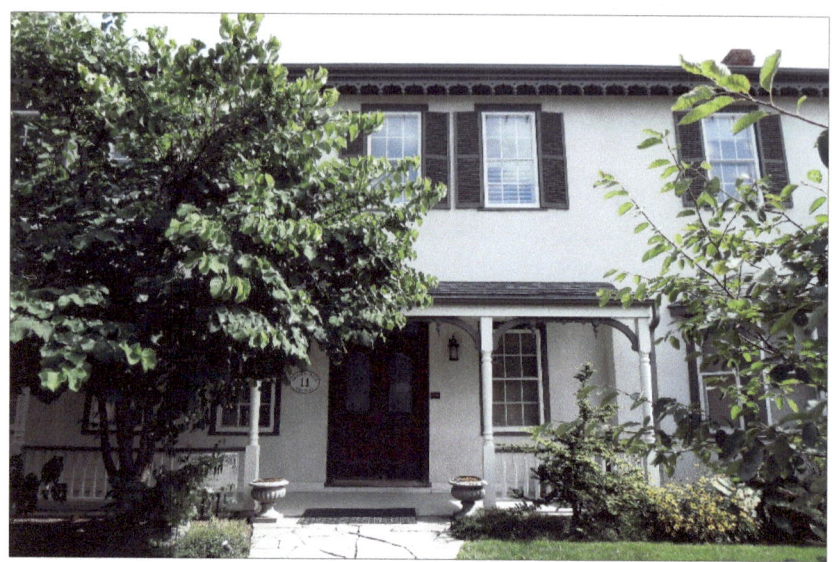

Notice the narrow double doors and the columns holding up the porch roof. The roof is ornamented with dentil blocks along the sill.

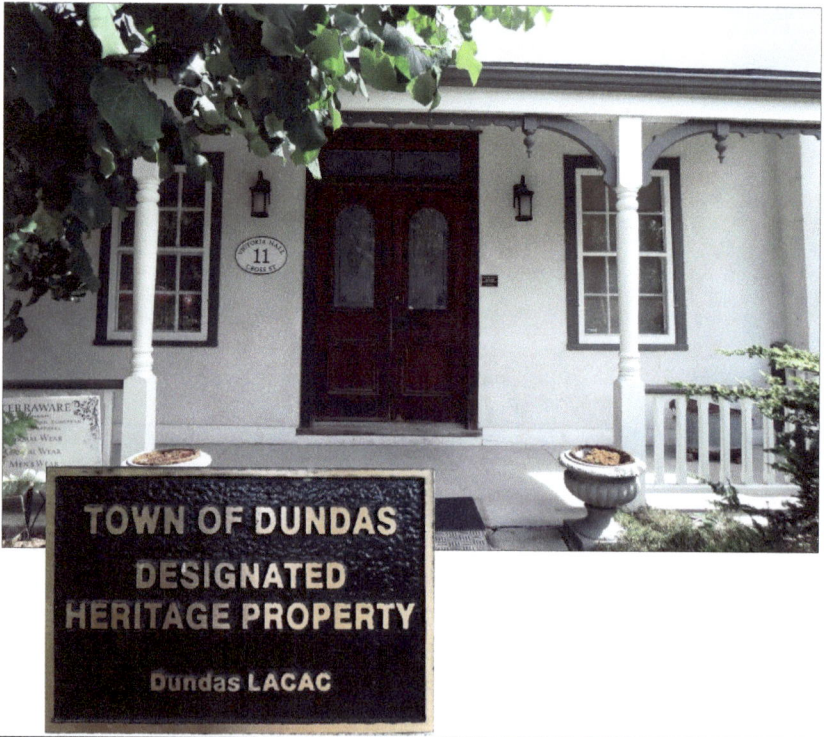

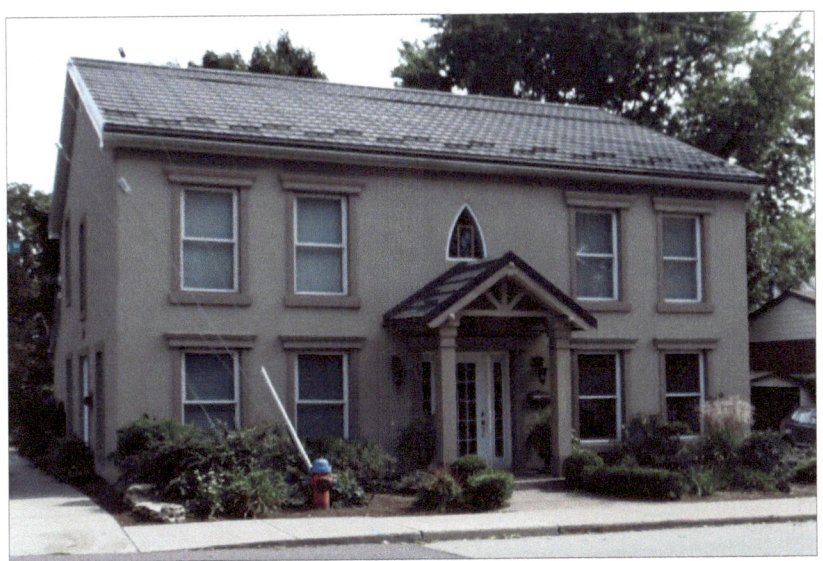

21 Cross Street has had a lot of renovations. The middle, second-story window is very unique.

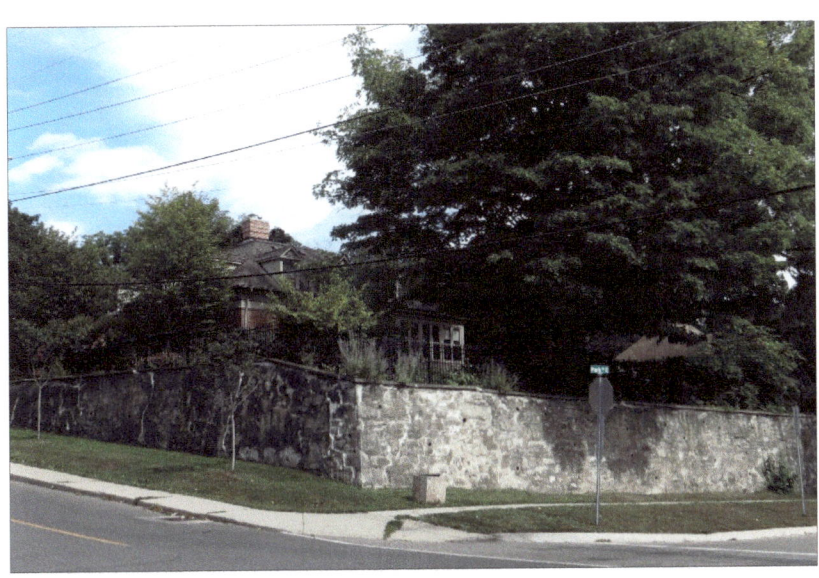

25 Cross Street has a wonderful stone wall, dormers, and bay windows.

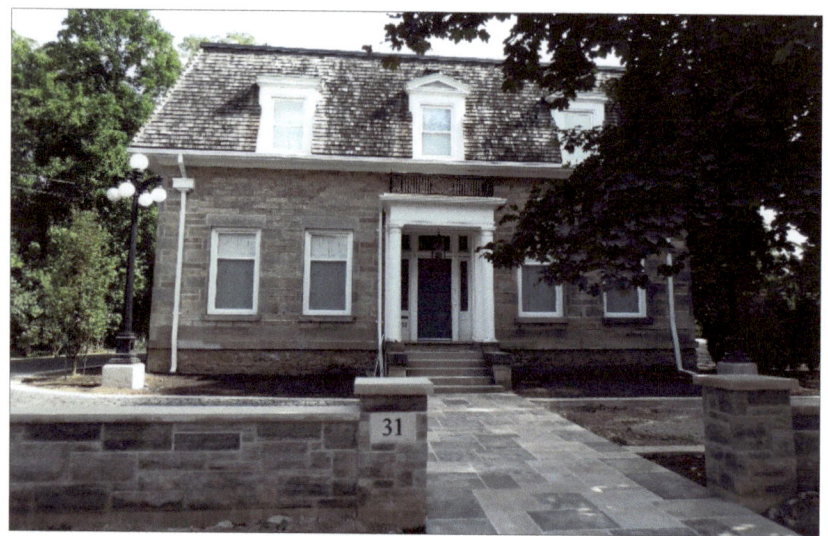

31 Cross Street has a second empire style with a mansard roof with Neoclassical style dormers. Note the iron cresting over the doorway

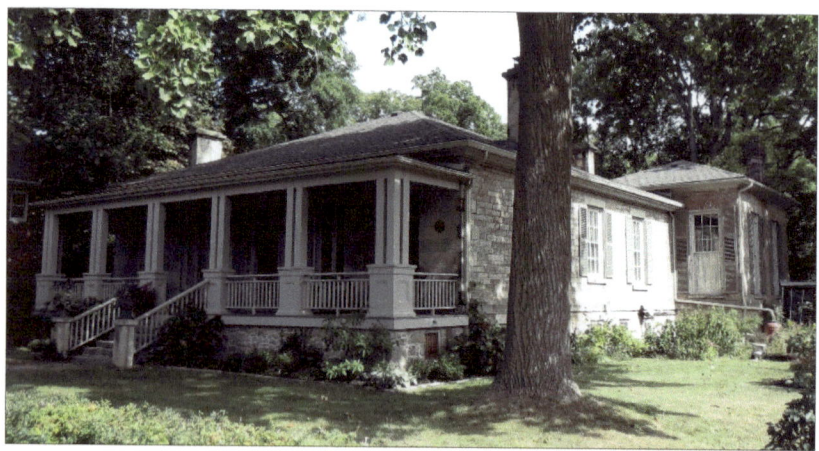

35 Cross St. is a Dundas heritage building with unique columns—3 square columns x 6.

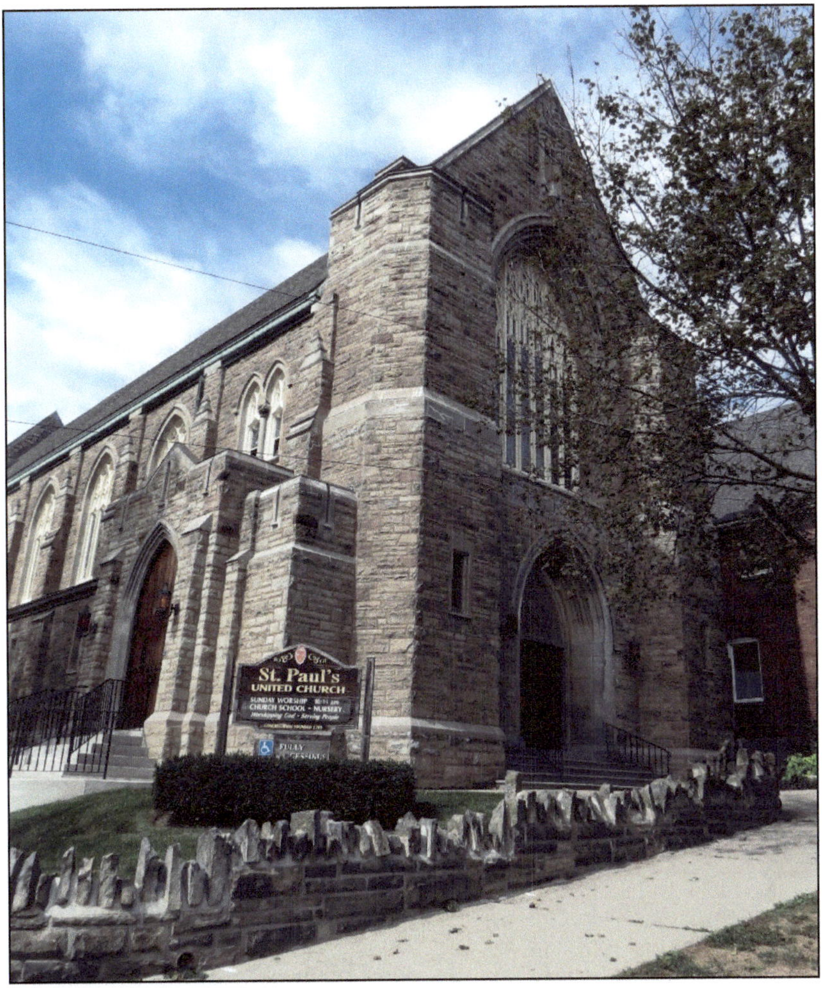

St. Paul's United Church on Cross St. has distinctive corner

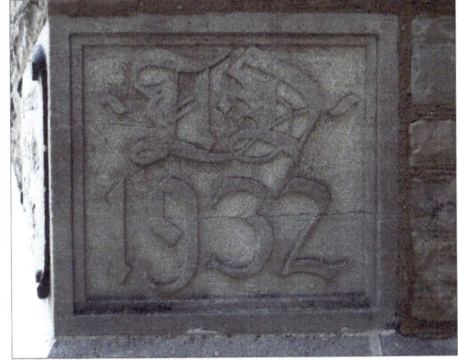

stones and gorgeous front door.

The congregation was formed in 1795, but the church was built in 1855, with another edition in 1932, as shown on this corner.

Barbara A. Fanson

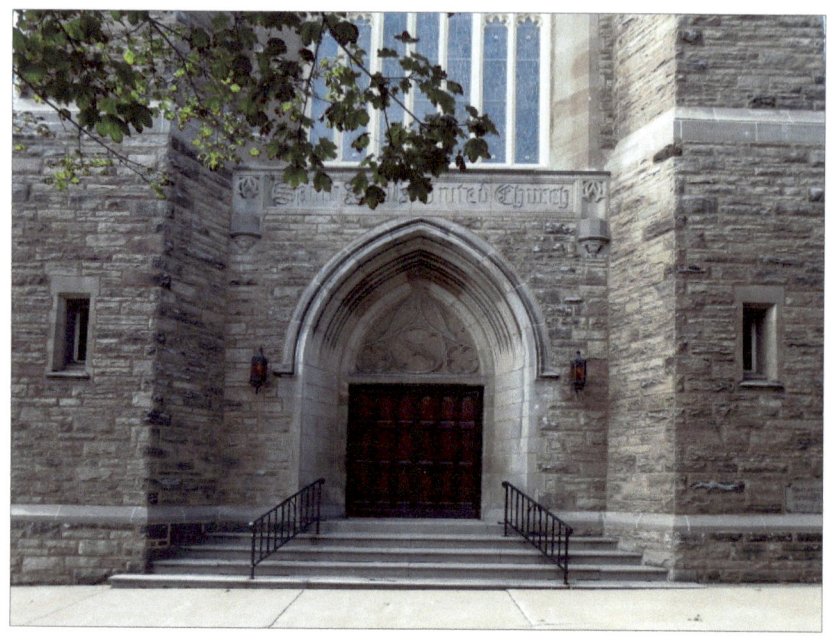

The Gothic Revival style has buttresses on the exterior of the church for support, and finials at the top for decoration.

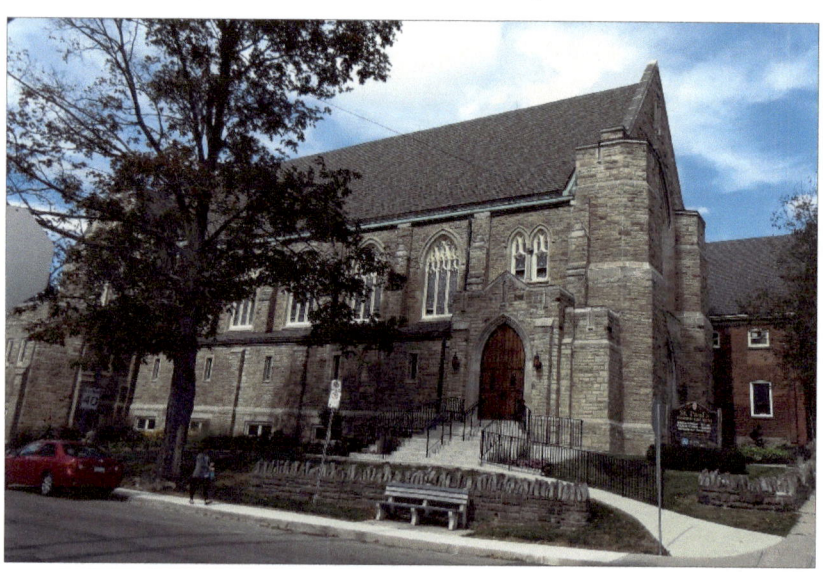

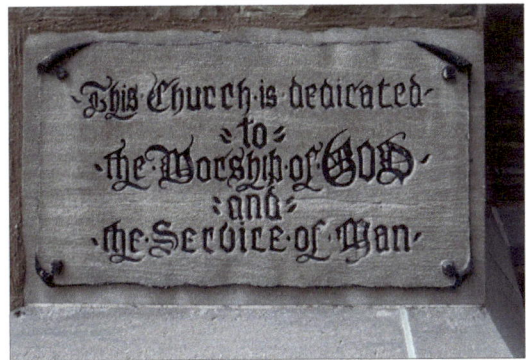

This church is dedicated to the Worship of God and the Service of Man.

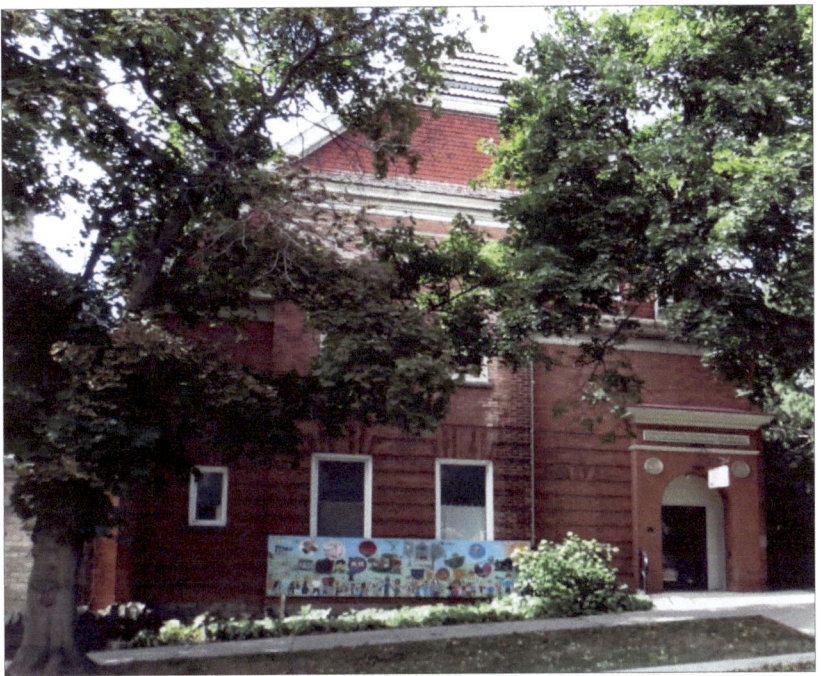

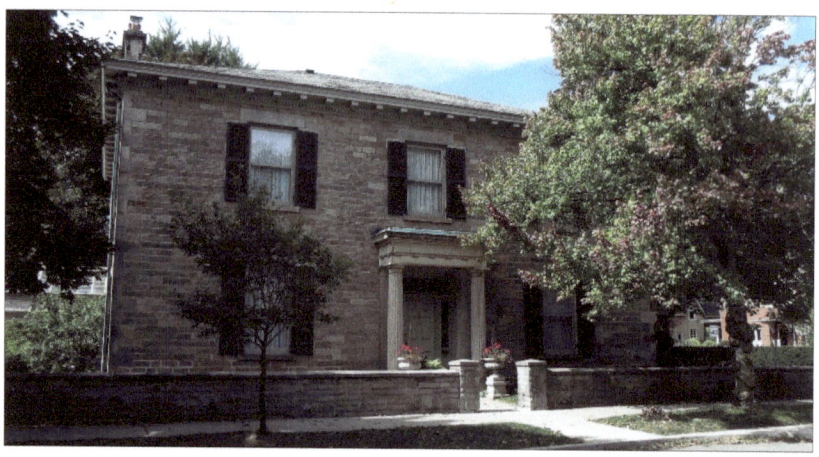

32 Cross Street is a Classical Revival with cut stone veneer. The three bay house has a hip roof ornamented with dentil blocks along the sill. The windows have concrete sills. arched windows, and a small roof above the front door.

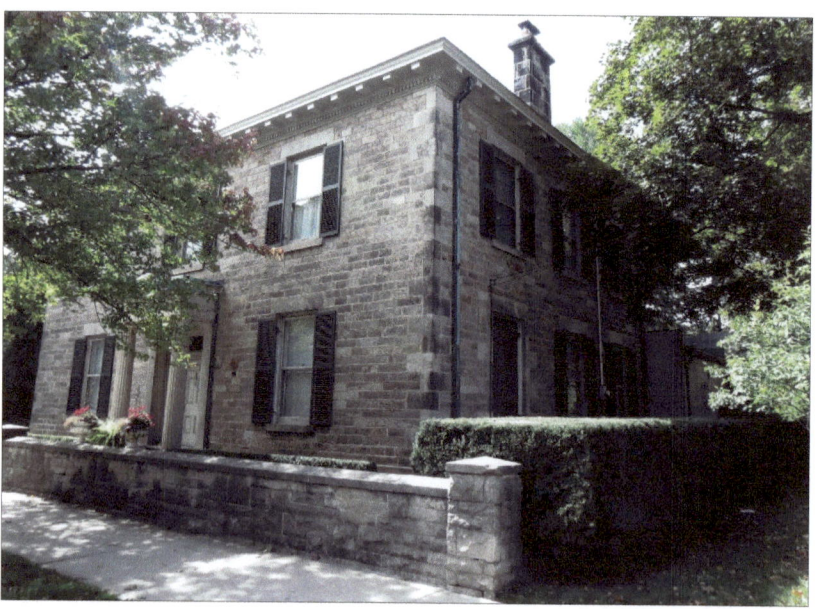

The corner of the house features stone quoined corners and brackets support the roof. This is a formal, solid building.

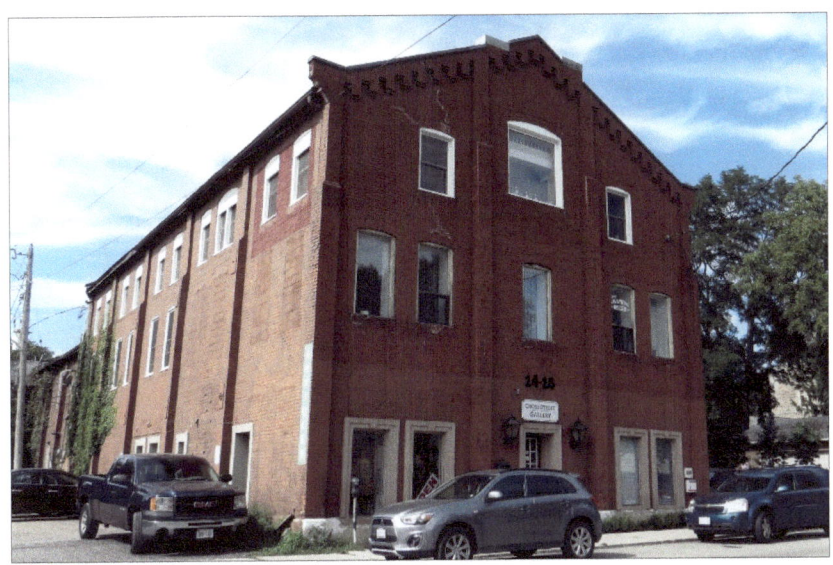

14-16 Cross Street is home to the Cross Street Gallery. The 3 story commercial building has fancy brickwork at the top of the front wall and you can see the original arched door.

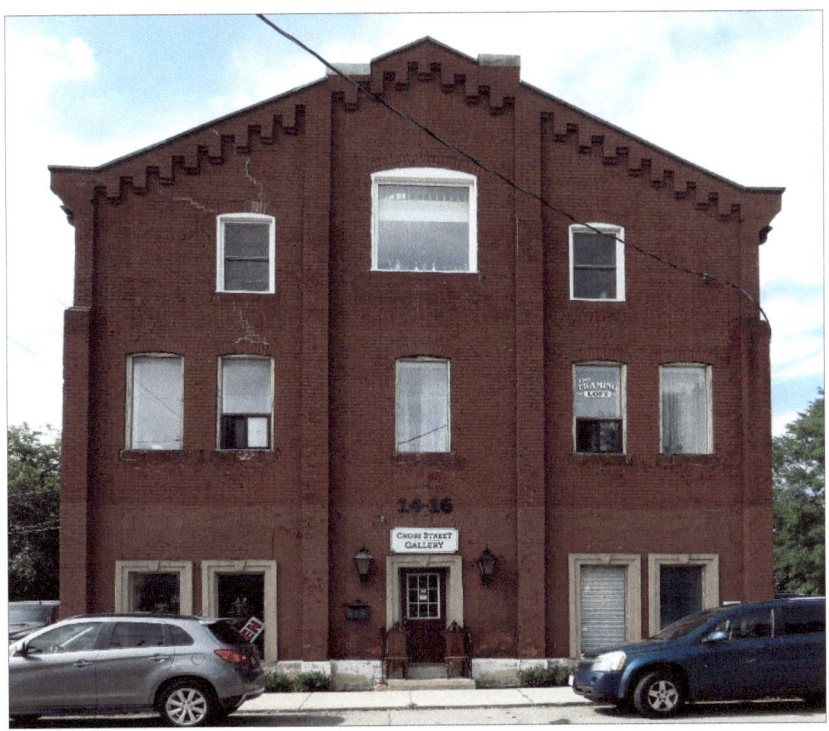

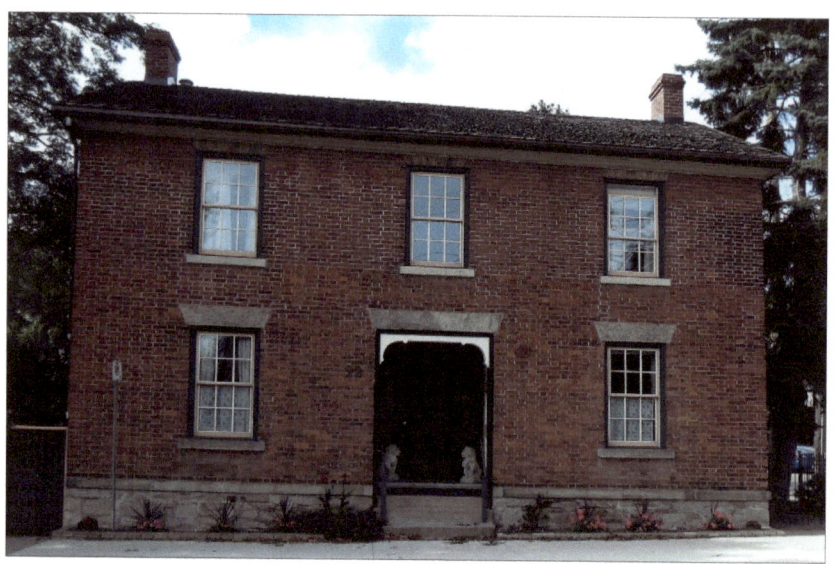

22 Cross Street is a classic two story house, built in the 1840s with 12 paned windows.

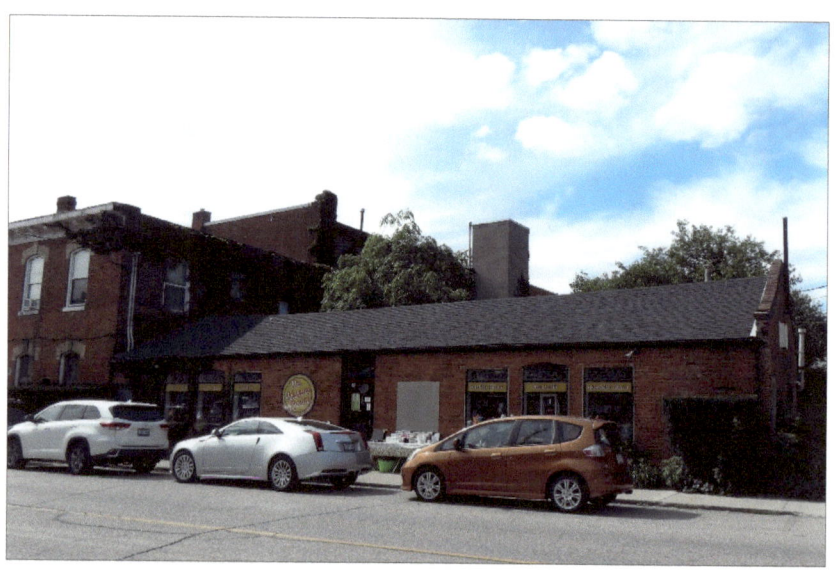

The Keeping Room occupies 6 Cross St. and 5 King St. W. Notice the hoods above the upper windows and the brackets under the roof.

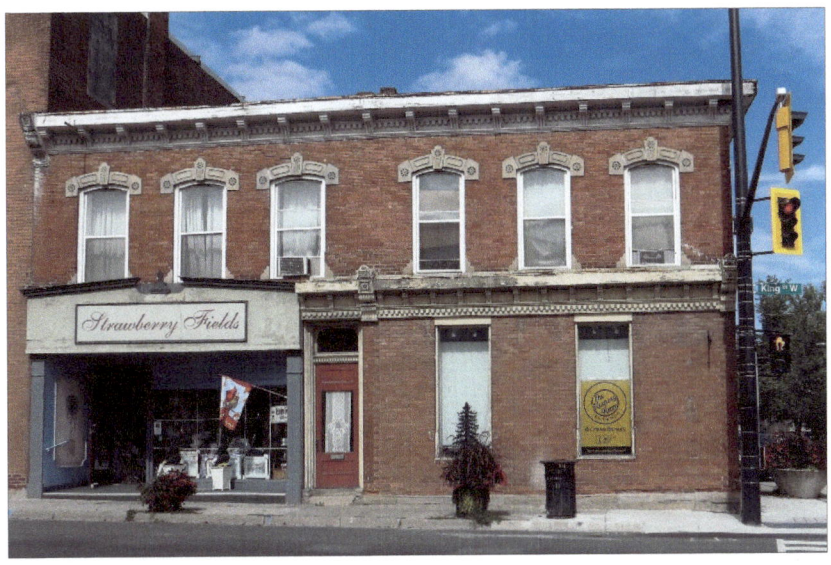

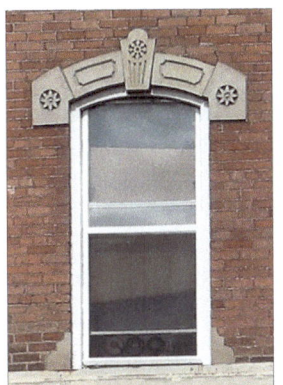

5 King St. W. is home to The Keeping Room on the right and Strawberry Fields at 7 King St. W. is on the left. The second-story windows have heavy, detailed hoods with a keystone in the middle. A decorative element was also added to the bottom of the windows. The door frame and door have a lot of detailing.

The Keeping Room is the toy store for cooks and chefs with kitchen supplies and utensils.

Strawberry Fields is a cute little shop selling wonderful gifts for those you love!

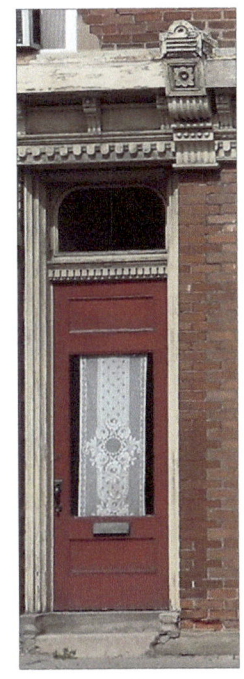

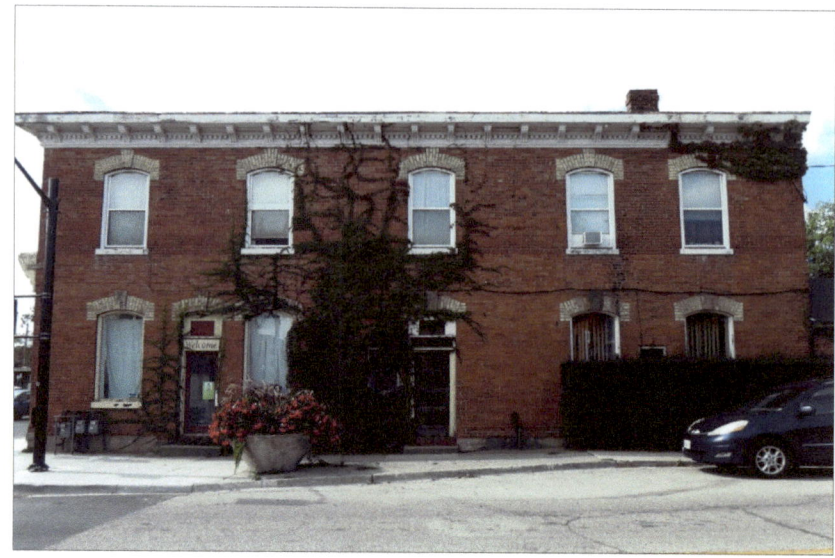

The East side of The Keeping Room on Cross St. is just as beautiful.

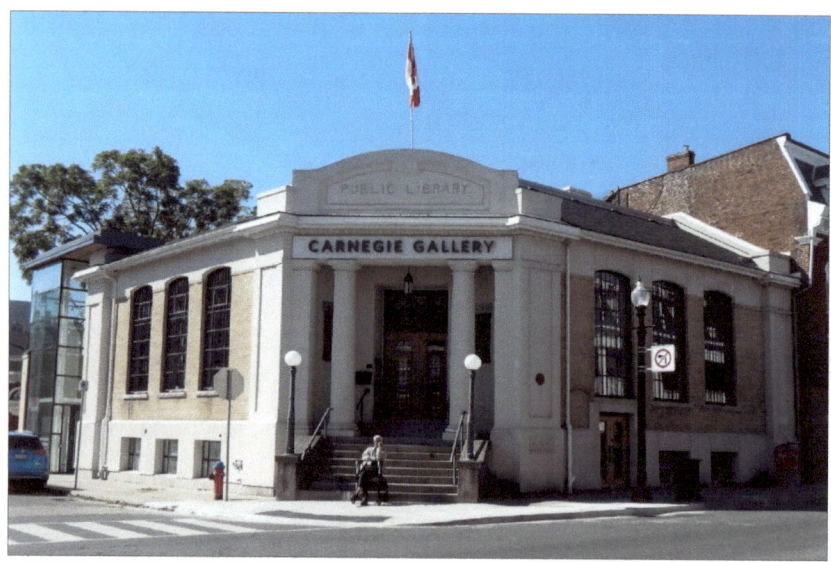

The Carnegie Gallery at 10 King St. W. is inside the 1910 Andrew Carnegie Library building, which was the town's public library. Notice the words "Public Library" in the pediment above the front door.

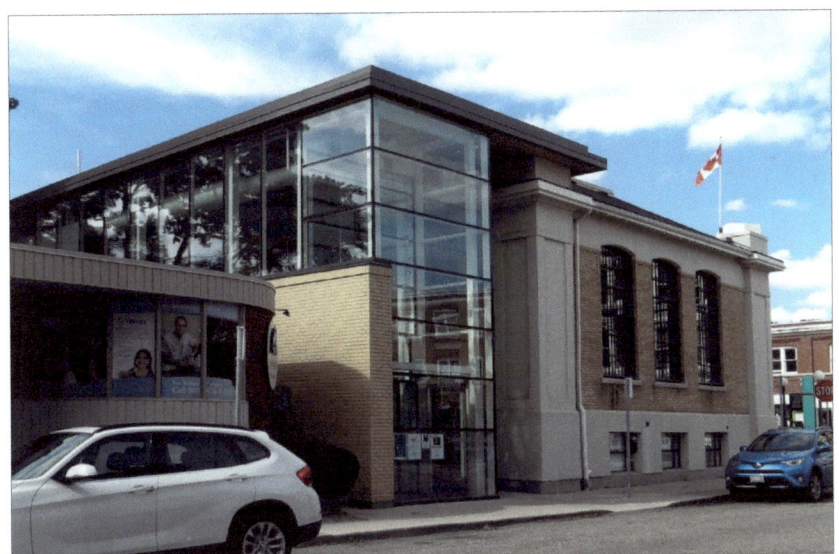

The building was officially opened on Dec. 8, 1910 as the town's first free public library.

The Carnegie building has exterior stairs with two classical columns supporting the portico, which are examples of the Beaux-Arts or neoclassical style used for other Carnegie-funded buildings. Notice the large symmetrically placed windows on the side.

In 2013, the Carnegie Gallery building was renovated and the glass addition on the back, but some architectural features have been designated under the Ontario Heritage Act (1980).

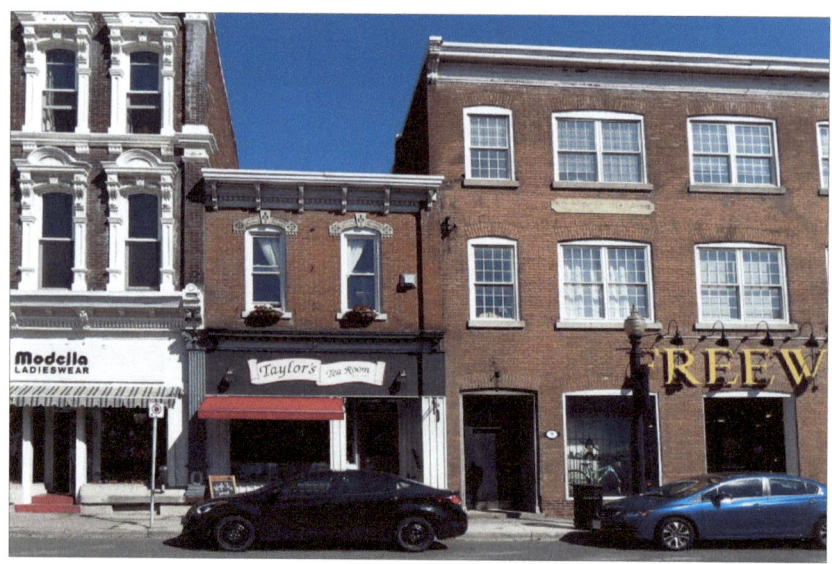

Freewheel Cycle at 9 King St. W. has the 12-paned windows on the second and third floor with arched brickwork. Freewheel Cycle is passionate about bikes.

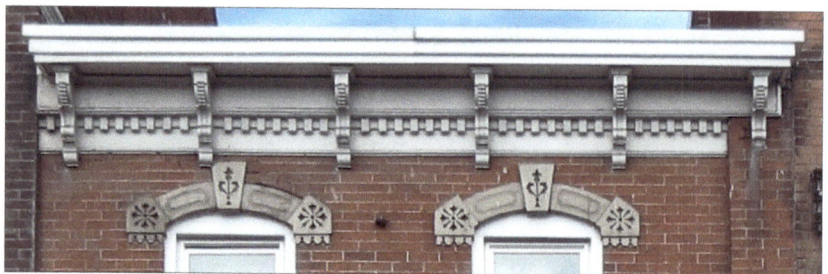

11 King St. W. is a two-story building with a beautifully designed cornice across the top, large, stone hoods and keystone above the upper story windows. Since 1993, Taylor's Tea Room has served up English-style cooking in a cozy atmosphere.

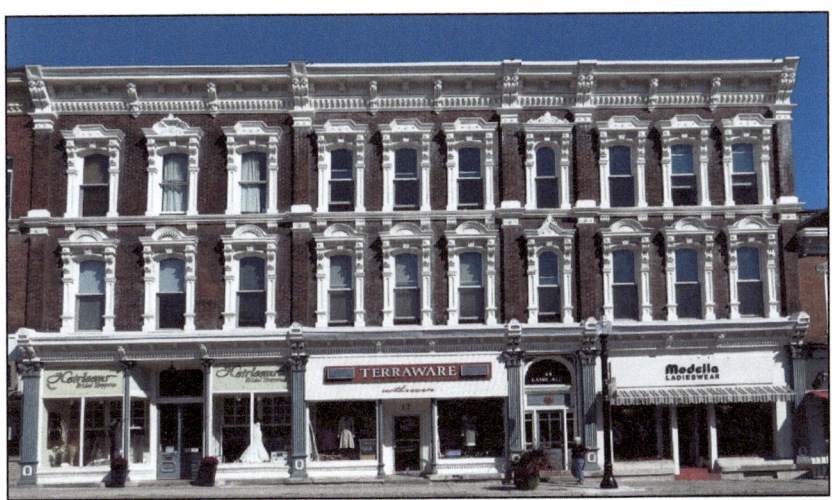

13 to 17 King St. W. is a wonderful example of an Italianate commercial block. The over-sized cornice, the capitals with their moulding, the window surround with the ornate brackets, pediment and acroterion, the dentils under the roof were made of cast iron, probably in a Dundas foundry.

Modella Ladieswear for the best-dressed woman occupies 13 King St. W.

Terraware Earthaware at 17 King St. W. has Canadian designed, European inspired quality apparel, ethically produced and environmentally conscious.

The author bought her wedding gown and veil at Heirloom Bridal Shoppe at 19 King St. W. Notice the details on the French double doors and under the large windows.

Built in 1883, 19 King St. W. used to be Hugh Walker's Hardware Store. Though it was renovated in 1987, the 14-foot ceilings, sliding rail ladder, long counter, and hardwood floors were retained.

Barbara A. Fanson

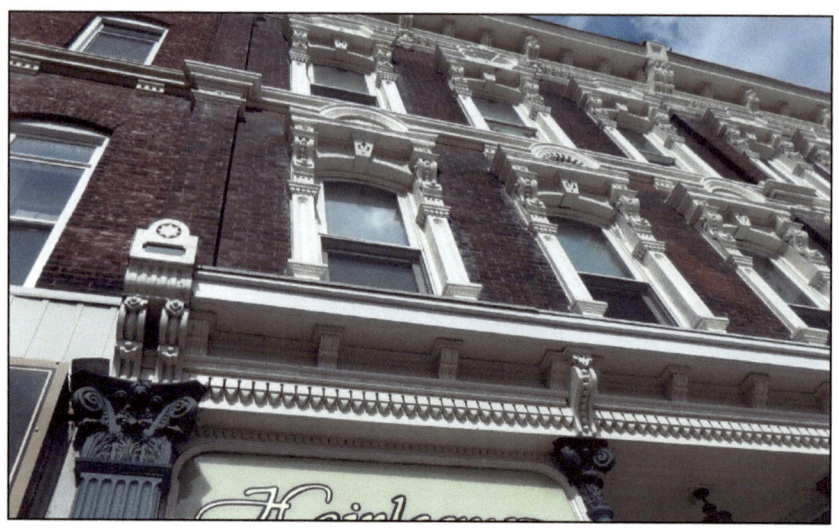

Look up to truly appreciate the decorative capital at the top of the column and exaggerated window hoods above the second-story windows.

In 1798 Ann Morden was given a Crown grant of land on the site of 13 to 19 King St. E. By 1868, the brick building at this site was owned by William Laidlaw, a tailor. In 1874, his widow Janet Laidlaw rented the storefront to John Rankin and then Thomas Seaman, clothiers. A fire on September 27, 1881 destroyed the buildings from Cross Street to the Collins Hotel.

Peter and Robert Laing were grocers and owners of the Wellington Block, which was east of Laidlaw's building. By 1882 the Laing brothers had rebuilt the former buildings of the Wellington Block, the Dufferin Hotel, and part of Janet Laidlaw's store.

The Laing Building was built in 1882 with the popular Italianate style, which displayed their wealth. A lot of pressed metal and cast iron was used to give the sculptured look to the façade. The buildings are separately owned but have the same look.

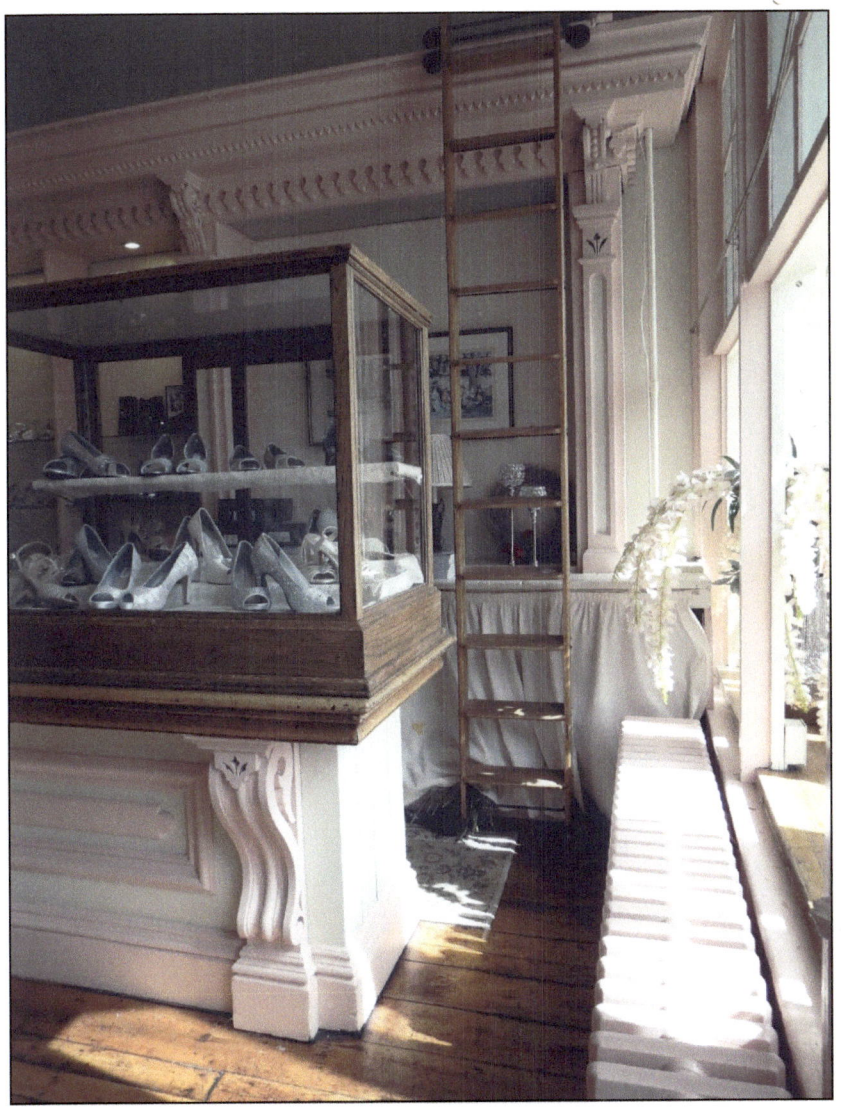

The inside of Heirlooms Bridal Shoppe has the same historical charm as the outside. The turn of the century building has 14' ceilings, intricate woodwork, original plank flooring, sliding ladder, and decorative counter and shelves.

T.H. McKenzie and J. Findlay Smith sold hardware in the Wellington Block before the fire.

In 1882 J. Findlay Smith moved his hardware store into the new Laing Building and starting a 95-year tradition. Later, Gordon C. Wilson and Hugh Walker also owned the hardware store.

About 1936 Hugh and Edith Walker bought the store at the western end of the Laing Block that they had previously rented. Hugh Walker's Hardware store was a Dundas landmark for more than 30 years until her retired in 1968.

By 1987 Heirlooms Bridal Shoppe had transformed the store into a bridal shop, but the interior still resembles the former hardware store.

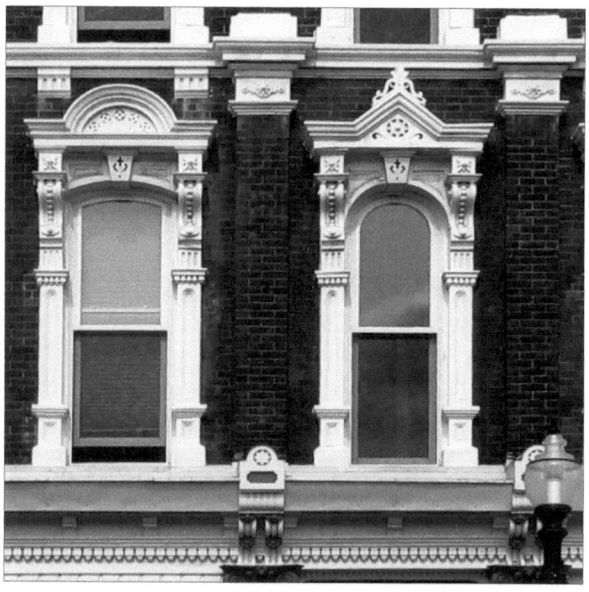

The block has oversized window surrounds and various pediment shapes above windows—some are pointed, some are arched.

The top cornice has ornamental double brackets and agraffes (decorative central keystone in an arch, often carved with a human face, cartouche or floral design.) This building also has pilasters (columns) on the sides of the doors and ornate mouldings.

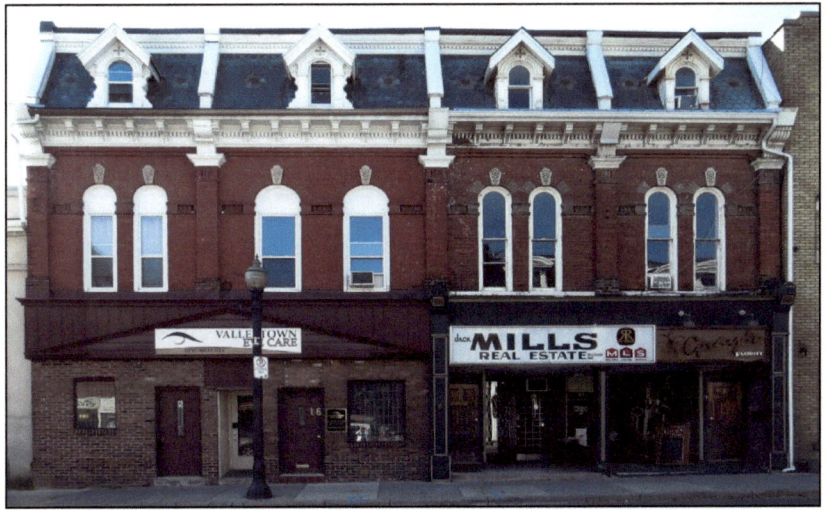

Look at the unusual roof shape at 14 to 22 King St. E. and distinctive shingles supported by brackets. It has four dormers and arched windows. Notice the keystone at the top of the arched windows on the second floor, flanked by a different coloured brick. The recessed door to Jack Mills Real Estate was typical of this period.

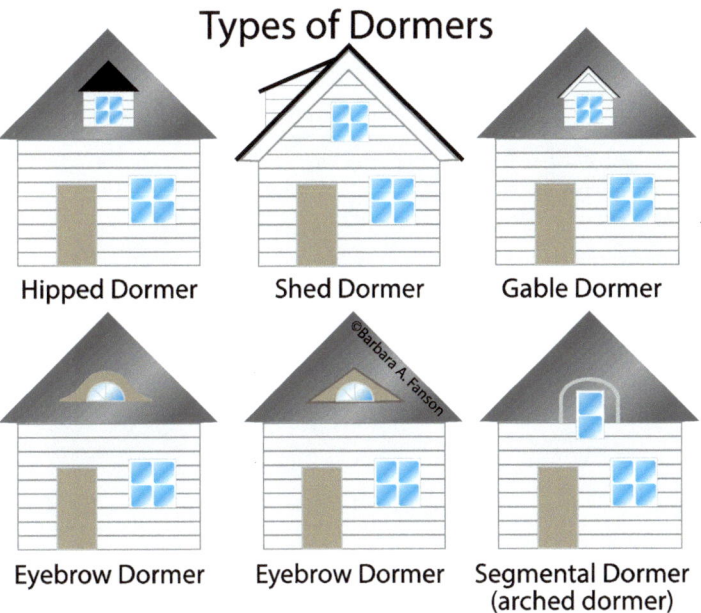

Barbara A. Fanson

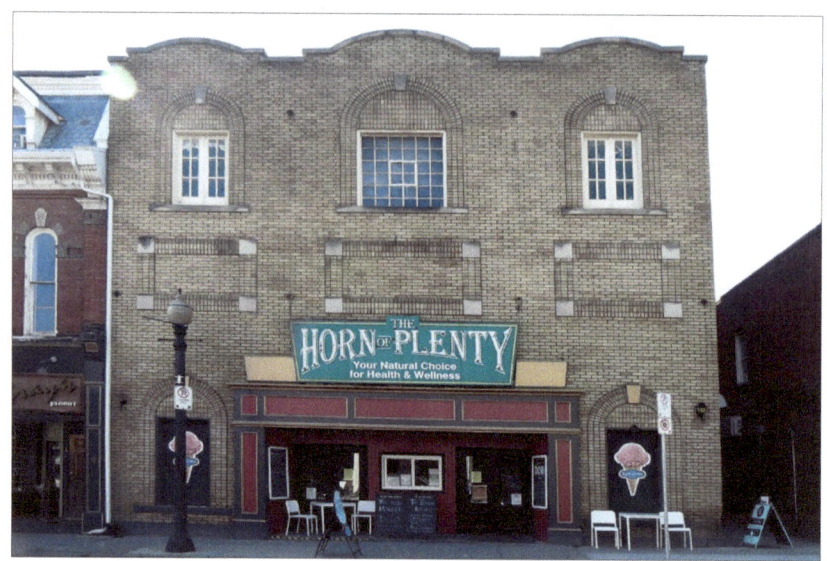

Notice the unusual façade of this light-coloured brick building at 24 King St. E., occupied by The Horn of Plenty. The building has brick arches above the windows with keystones and muntins on the windows separating the windowpanes, but it's the unusual curve at the top of the façade, that is the real eye-catcher.

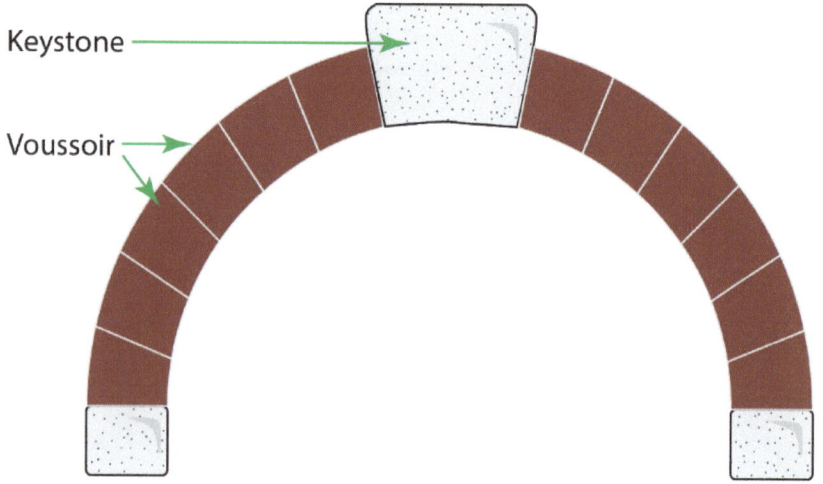

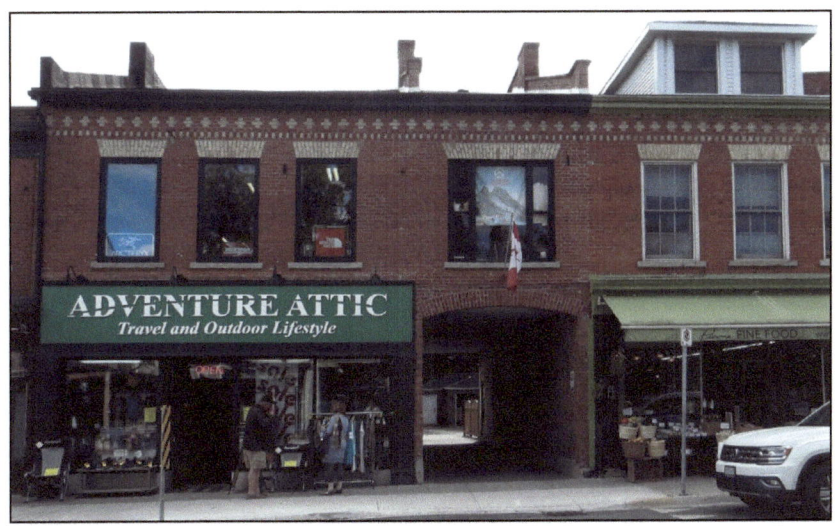

Notice the dichromatic brickwork of two colours at 28 and 34 King St. W. and the arched entrance to parking behind the building. Although it looks narrow, a horse and carriage would have fit through.

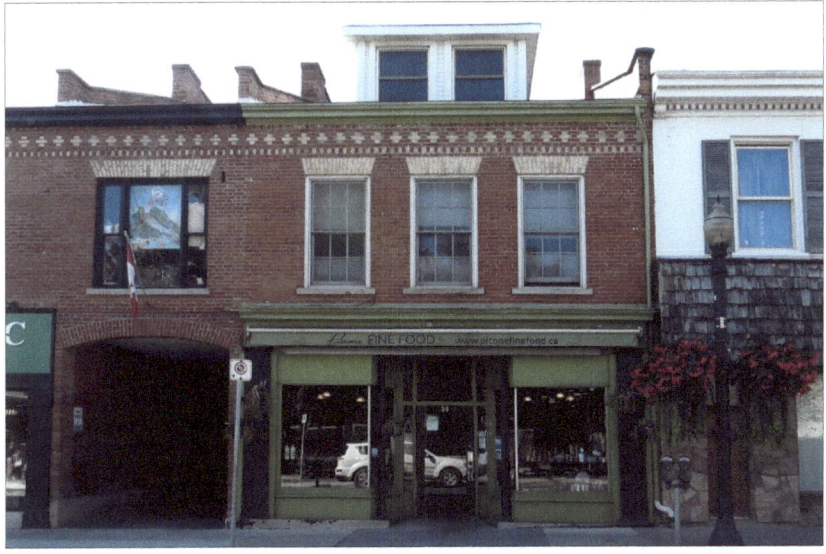

Picone Fine Foods at 34 King St. E. is the only building on King St. with that style of dormer. Look at the beautiful crosses in the brickwork at the top of the building.

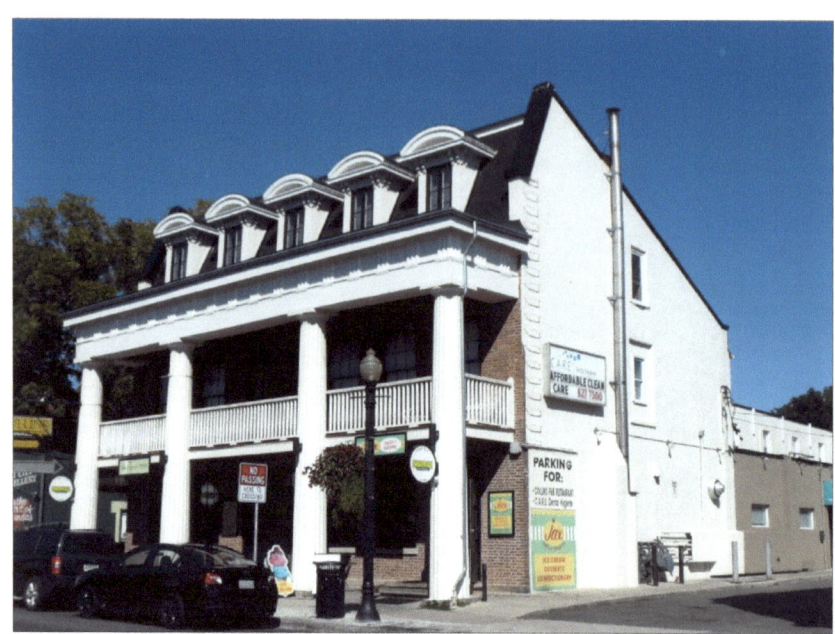

The Collins Hotel at 33 King St. West is the longest running hotel in Ontario, providing good food and service since 1841. The Classical Revival style boasts a front portico with the four fluted Doric columns with the triglyphs and metopes found on traditional Doric columns. The columns support a distinctive cornice. On the roof there are five dormers with Florentine pediments. The second floor of the hotel has a balcony running the full length of the building.

In 1833, the Collins family from Ireland settled in Dundas.

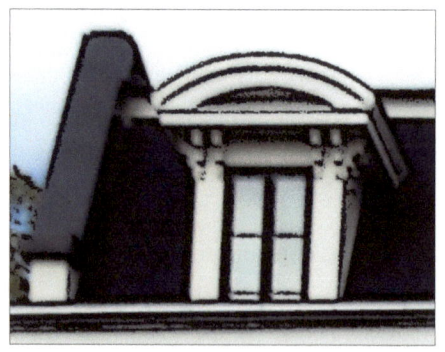

Within 5 years, Bernard Collins owned a successful saloon along the main downtown strip. In 1841 the Collins Hotel was erected across the street. Today, it is Collins Brewhouse.

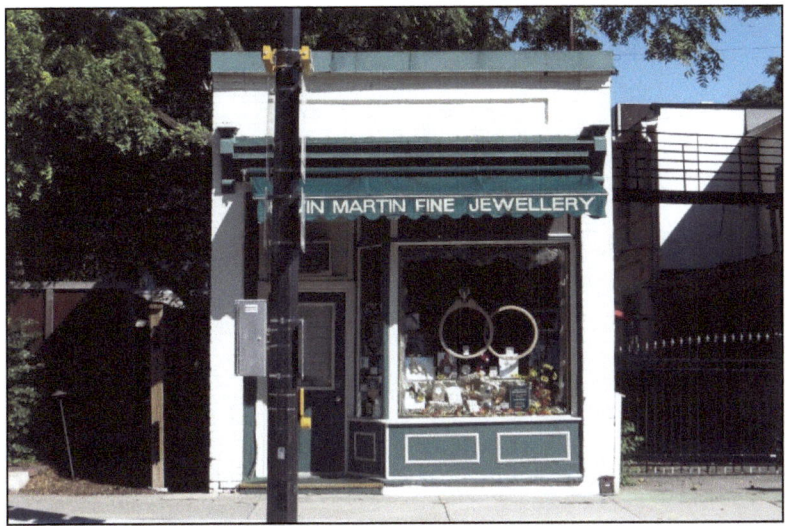

There are only a few one-story buildings in downtown Dundas like Kevin Martin Fine Jewellery at 37 King St. W.

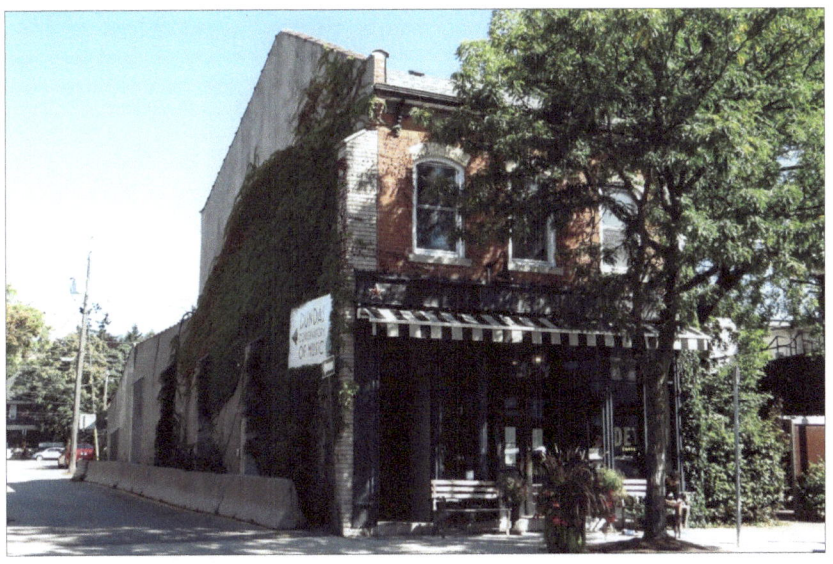

Detour Café at 41 King St. W. also has the beautiful arched windows.

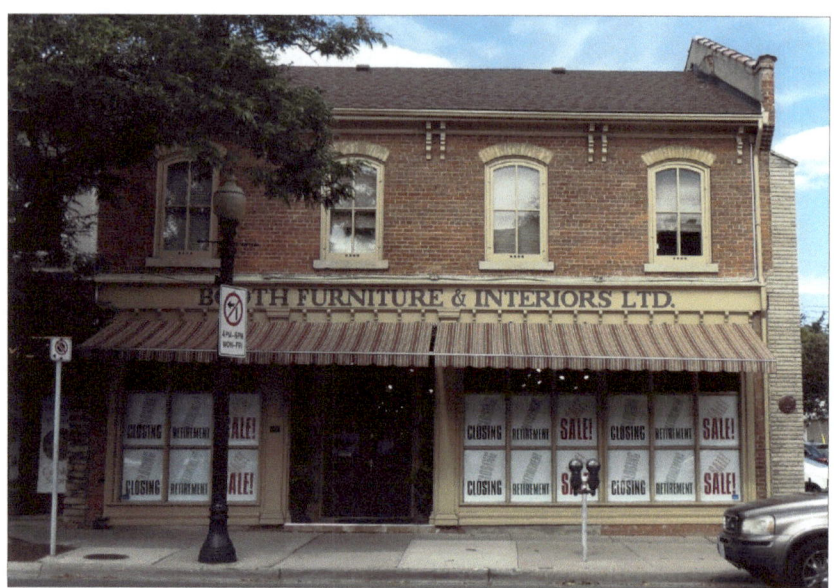

Booth Furniture & Interiors at 49 King St. W. has classic arched windows with dichromatic brickwork above the window (2 colours of brick), as well as double brackets under the roof.

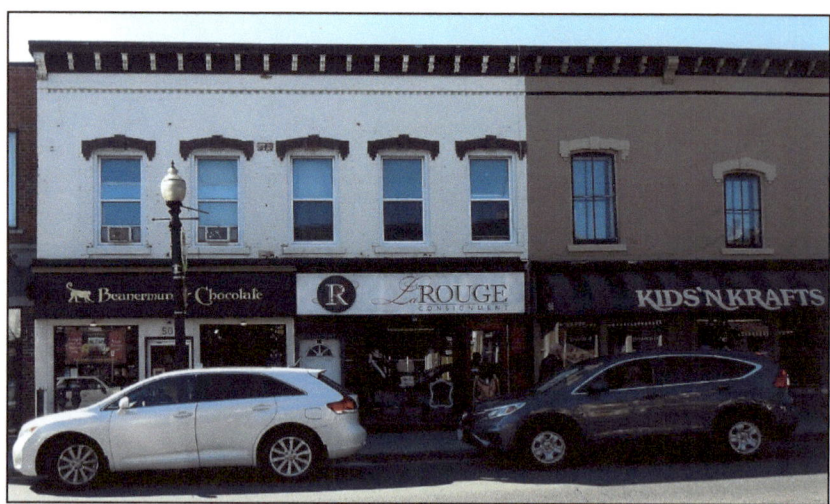

50 to 56 Main St. W. features Beanermunkey Chocolate, La Rouge, and Kids N' Krafts. The building has been painted to feature the window hoods and brackets along the cornice.

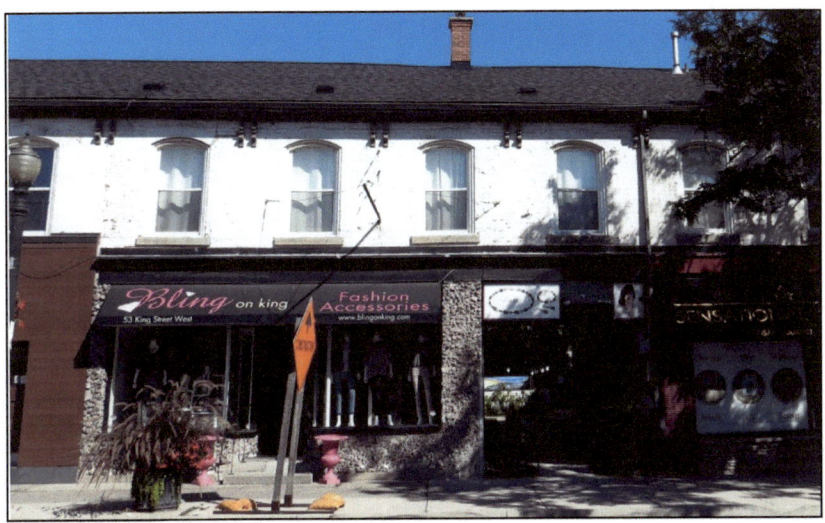

Bling on King occupies the ground floor of 53 King St. W. The second story has arched windows and double brackets supporting the roof.

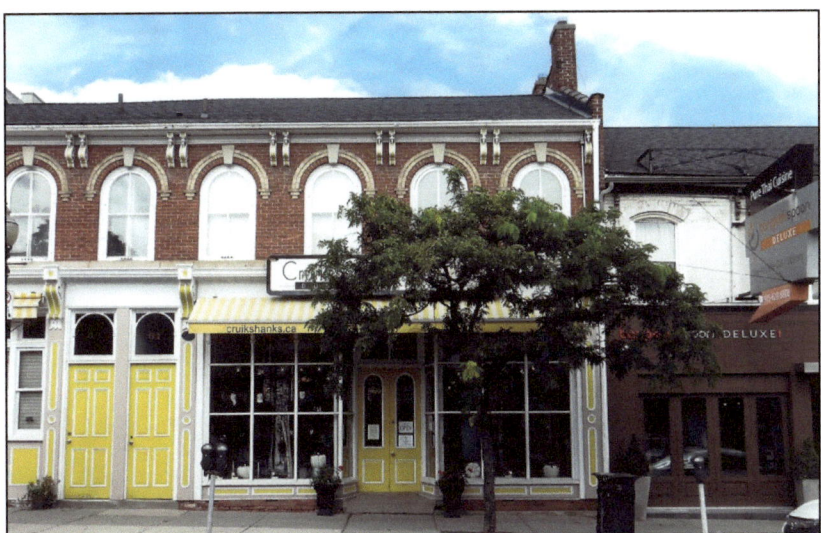

The De Luxe Restaurant at 57 King Street West was a nostalgic 1950s-style diner that closed in the 1970s and used in several film shoots. Today, it is the Bangkok Spoon Deluxe, a Thai restaurant.

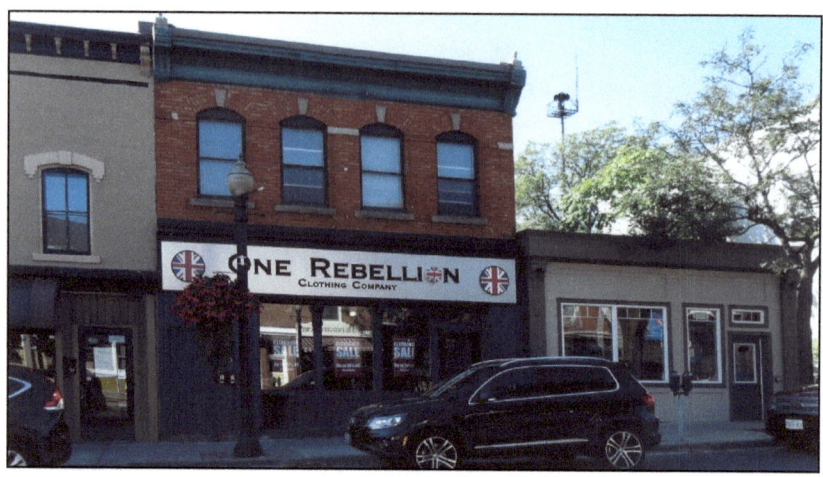

Look above One Rebellion at 60 King St. E. at the roof and you'll notice finials, the fancy ornaments. You can also see a keystone above the windows and voussoirs, an arch made of bricks, typical of the 1840s and 1850s.

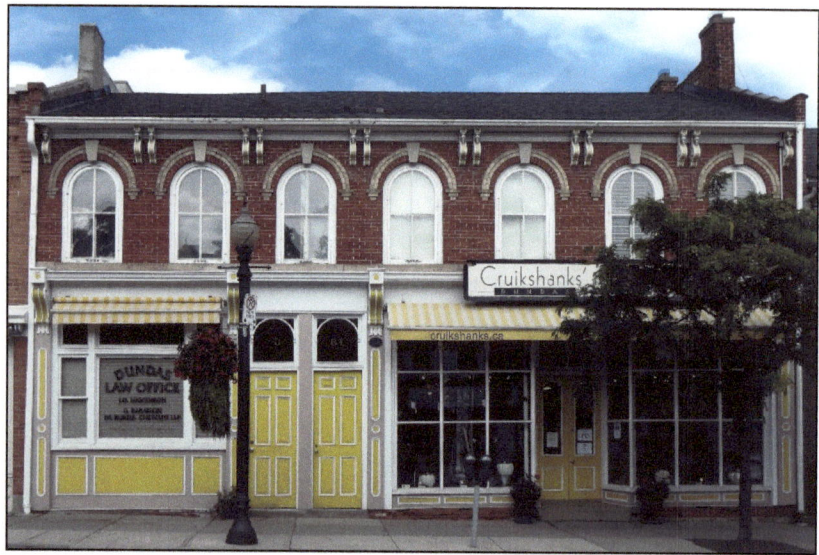

61 & 63 King St. is an example of an Italianate commercial block. With dichromatic bricks (two colours), arched windows with brick hood moulds, and double brackets under the roof, this building houses two businesses.

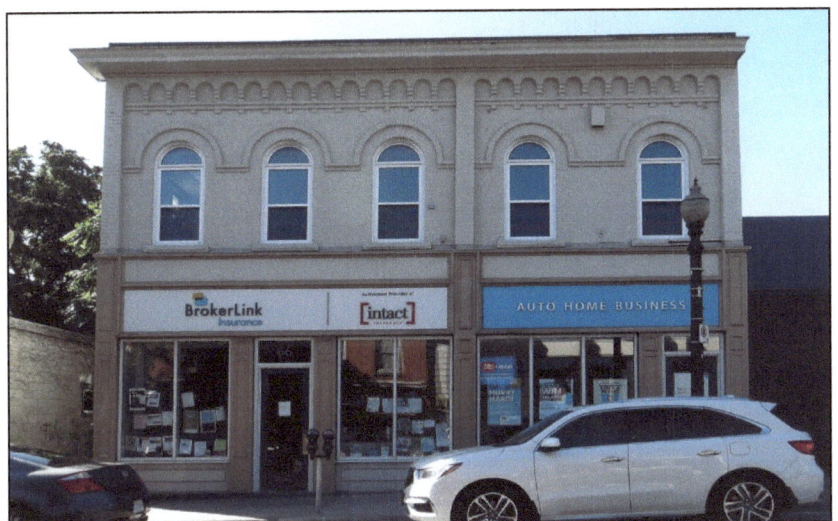

Brokerlink Insurance occupies 66 King St. W. with its elaborate brickwork and fancy cornice along the top.

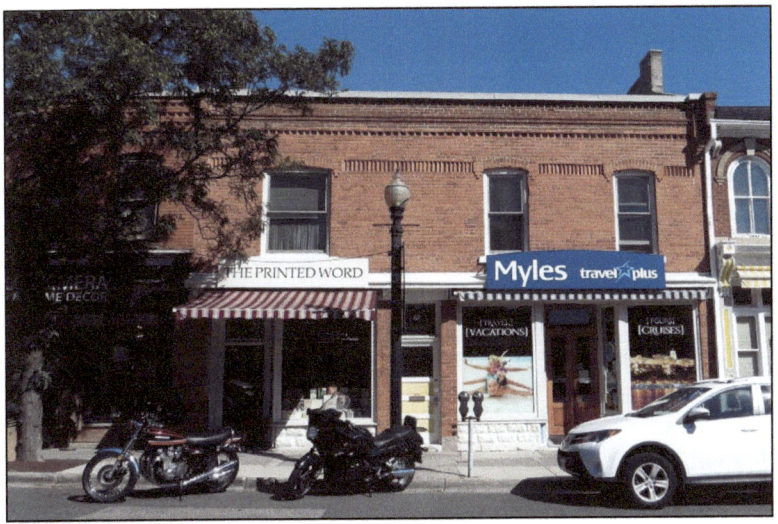

The Printed Word bookstore, which occupies 69 King St. W., sells poetry, religion, philosophy, fiction, and children's books. Myles TravelPlus at 65 King St. W. will help you book cruises, tours, and other travel destinations. Notice the fancy brickwork at the top of the façade.

Barbara A. Fanson

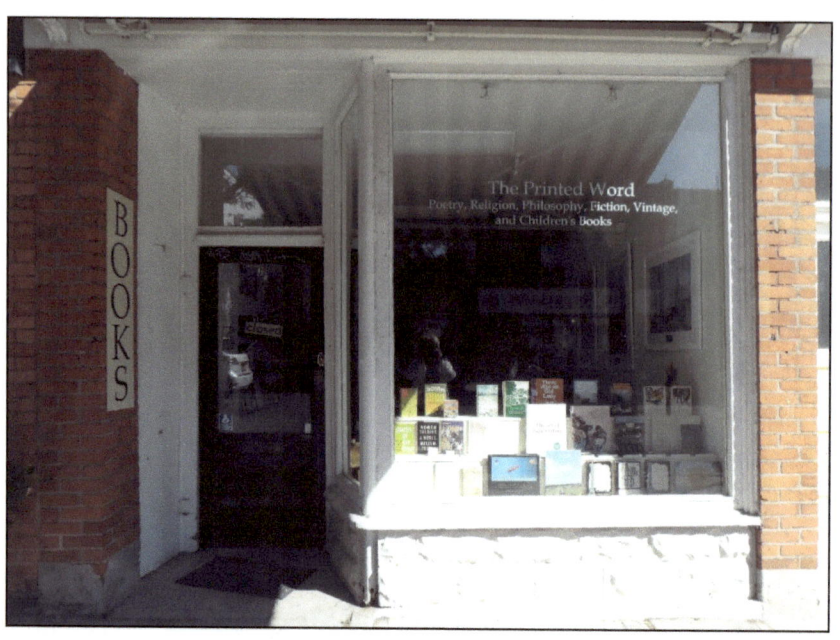

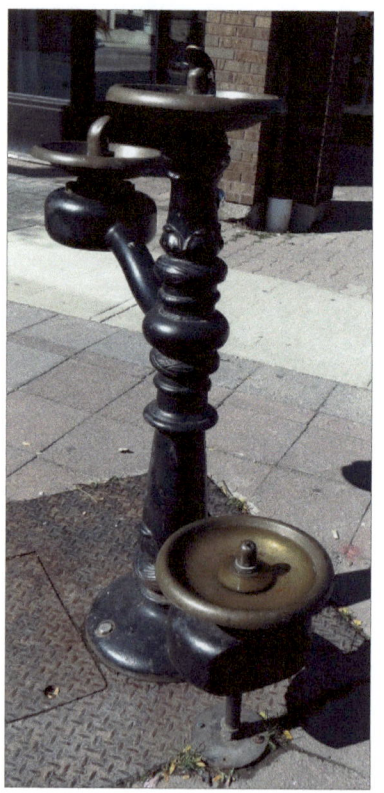

Notice the recessed entrance of The Printed Word, which was typical for retail stores during this period.

Built by Murdock, the water fountain was moved to the parkette next to Canada Trust at 82 King St. W.

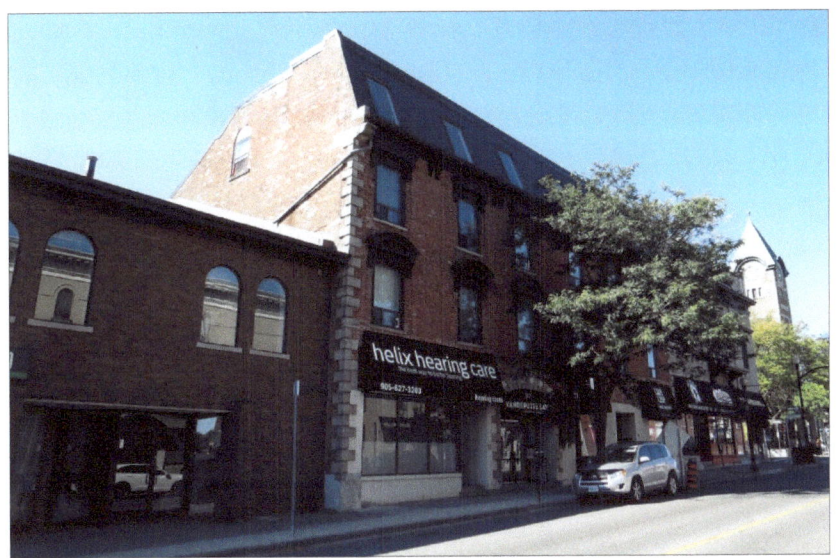

Helix Hearing Care, Vandeputte Law, and West Bayrouth Mediterranean Café are three of several businesses in the four-story building at 92 – 96 King St. W. Notice the odd-shaped roof. The building has lighter-coloured stone quoins on the corner, double brackets under the cornice, and heavy window hoods.

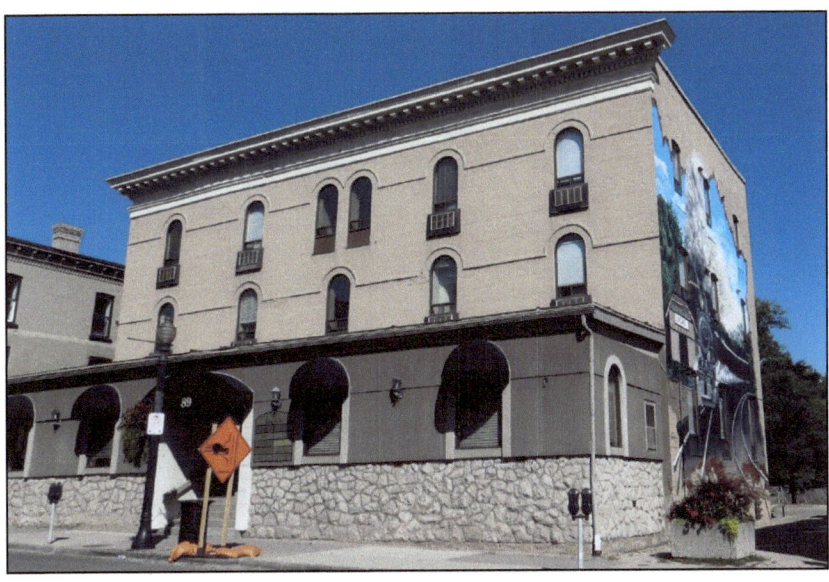

Barbara A. Fanson

89 King St. W. has arched windows and brackets at the top of the wall. Although the building has been painted, it still has much of the features popular in that period.

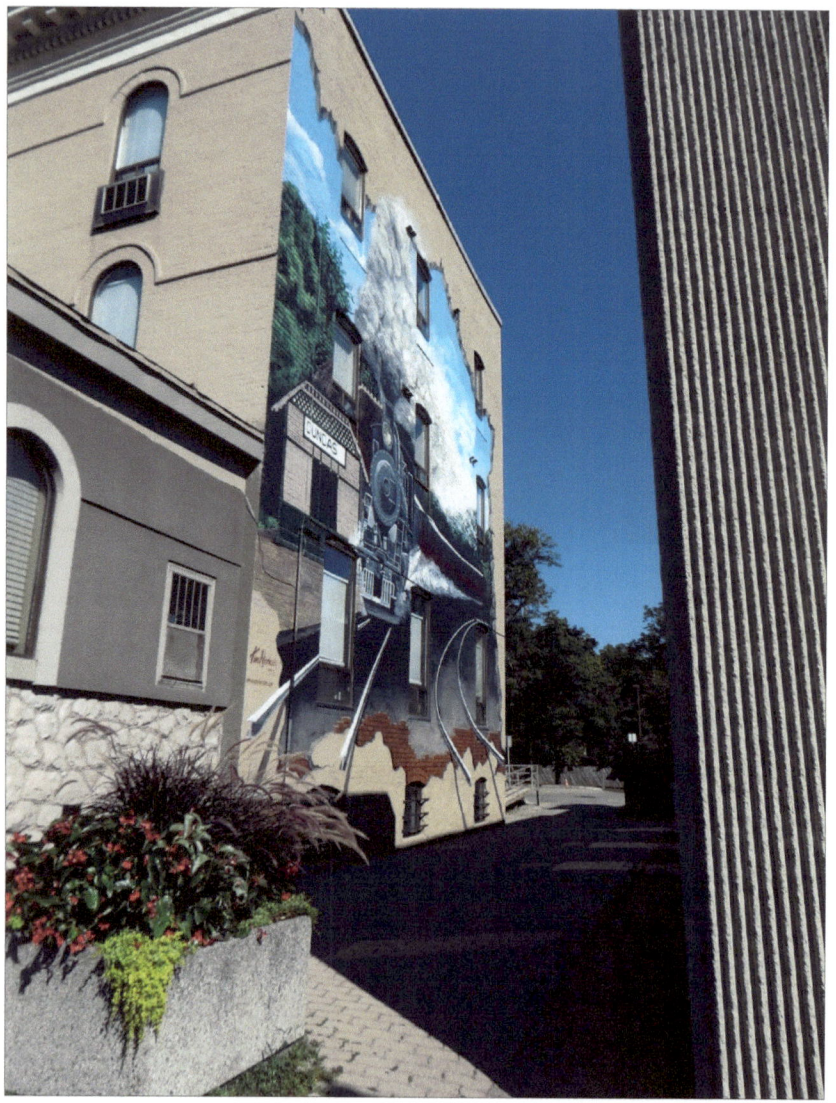

Tim Nÿenhuis of NineHouseProductions.com painted a mural on the wall in the alley in September 2017 on 89 King St. W.

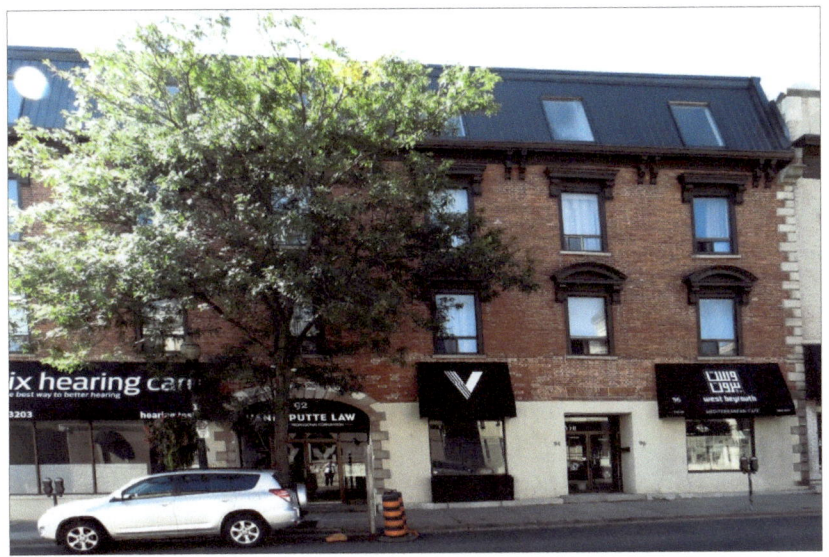

92 – 96 King St. W.

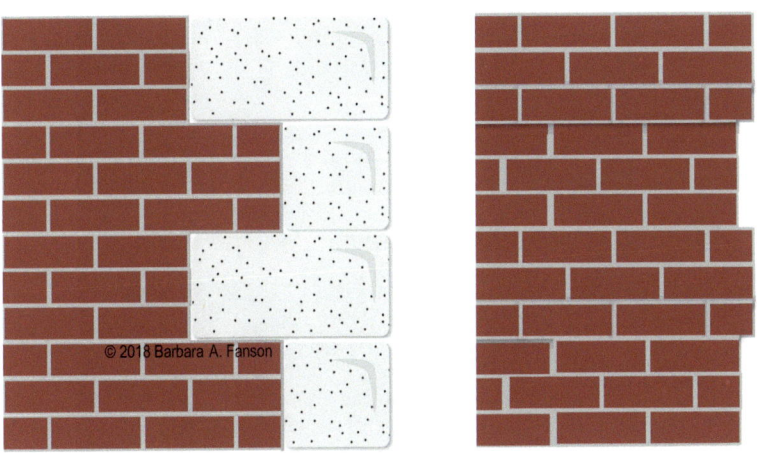

Quoined or Fancy Corners

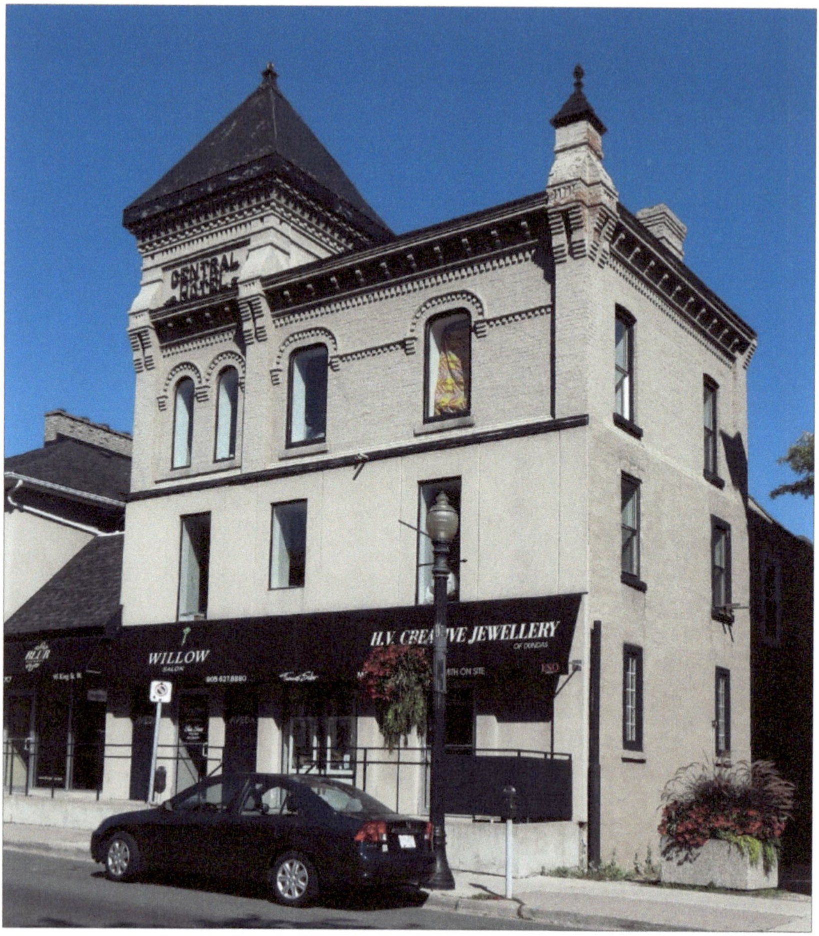

Originally the Central Hotel at 93 King St. W., the building is now home to HV Creative Jewellery, Willow Salon, and Blur Eyewear. Notice the beautiful brickwork near the top of the building and the arched windows.

Several buildings feature double brackets supporting the cornice.

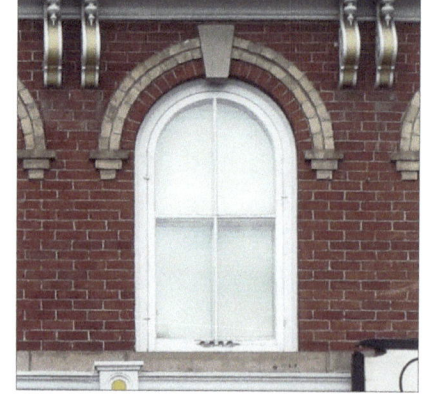

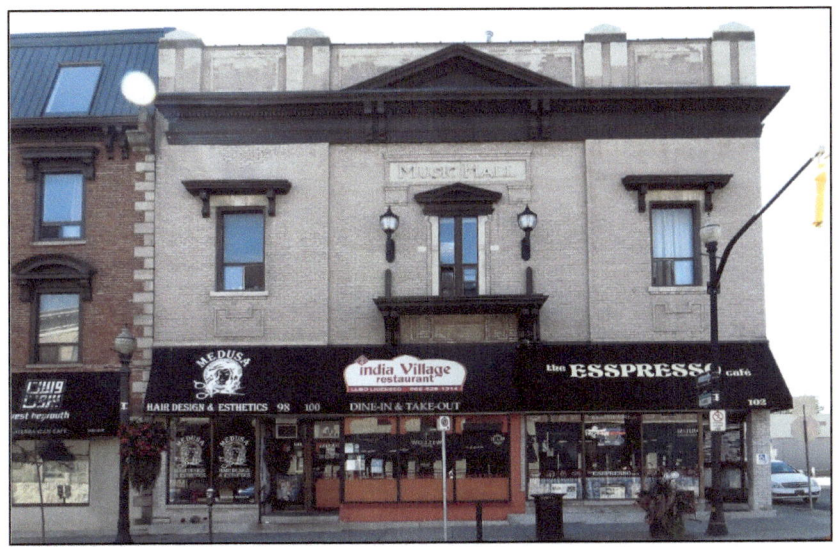

The Music Hall has 3 businesses: Medusa Hair Design & Aesthetics at 98, Indian Village at 100, and The Esspresso Café at 102. You can see the words Music Hall above the door. This building features several window hoods above the main door, windows, and also at the top of the façade.

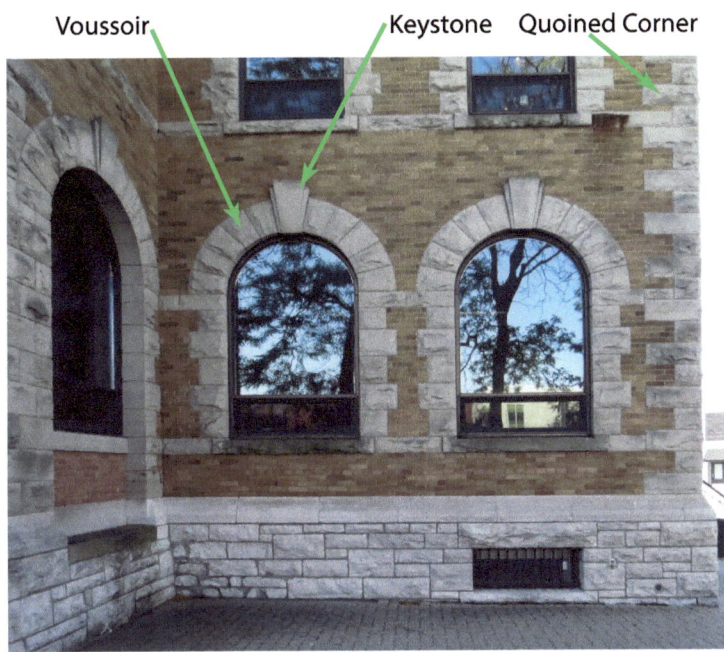

Barbara A. Fanson

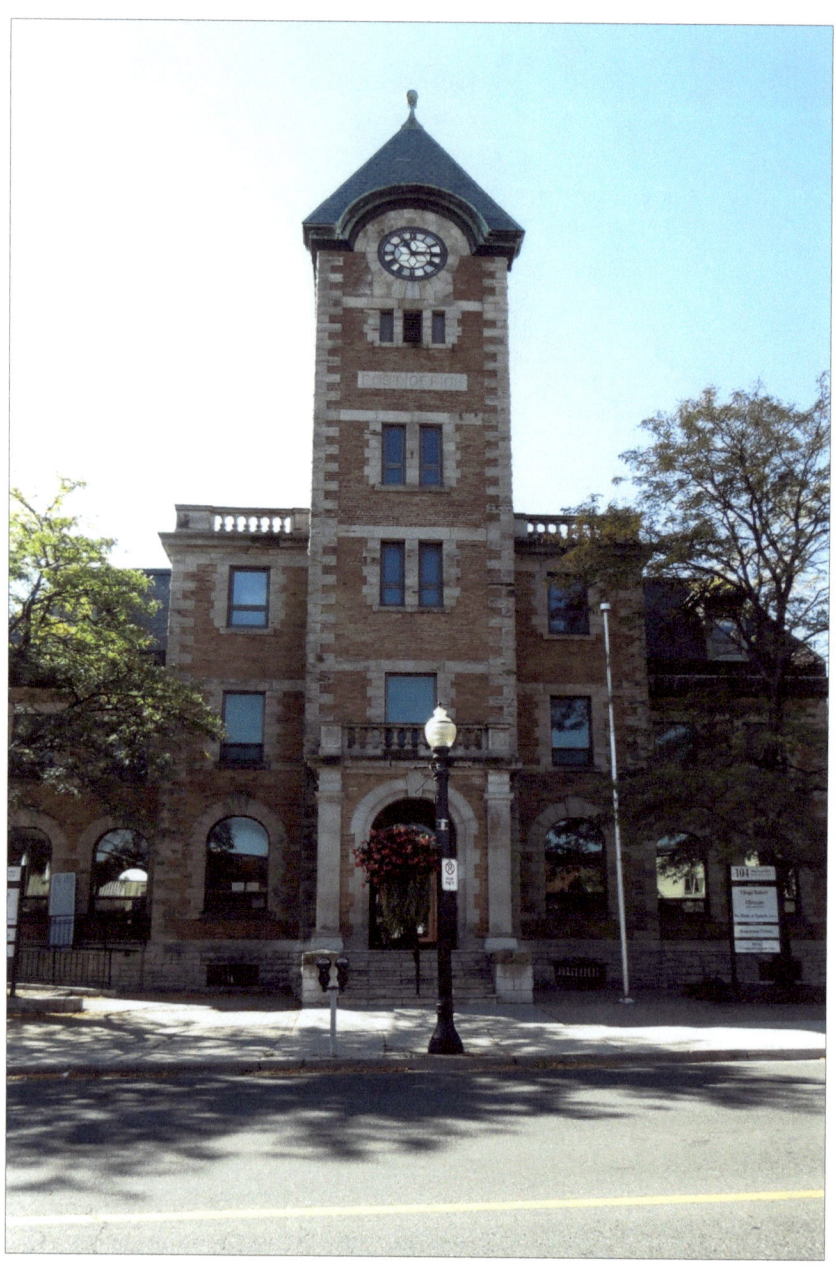

The Post Office at 104 King St. W. has a tall clock tower. Built in 1913 with a Romanesque façade featuring a 100-foot clock tower. The clock measures six feet across!

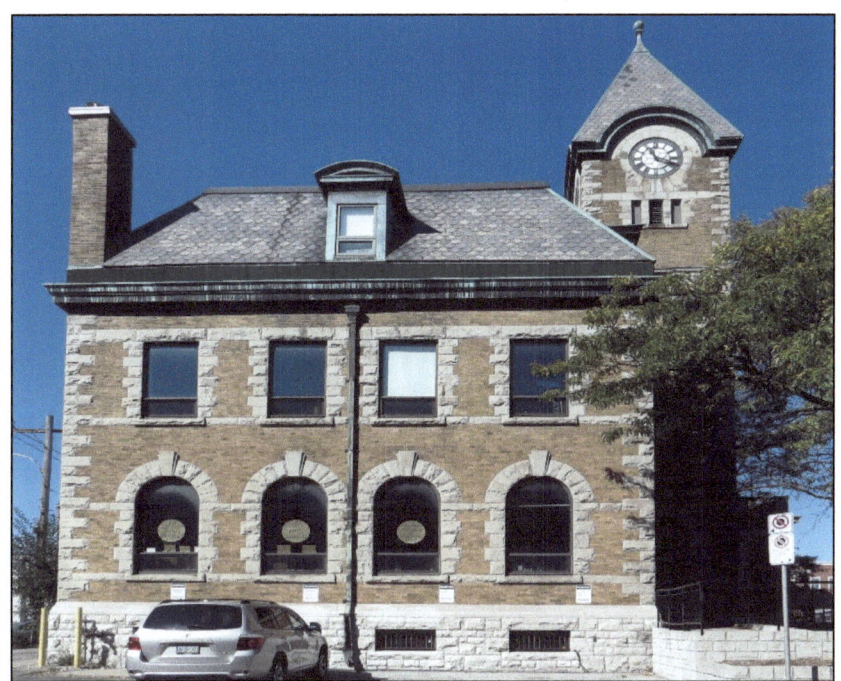

The grand, symmetrical building with large arched windows has a keystone at the top of the arch, surrounded by voussoirs to form the arch.

With several balcony rails and quoined corners, this is an outstanding commercial building with many unique features. Quoins are blocks at the corner of a wall, which could be a different colour or protruded. Sometimes, they are used to add strength to the wall, to add fancy corners, or to give a permanent impression.

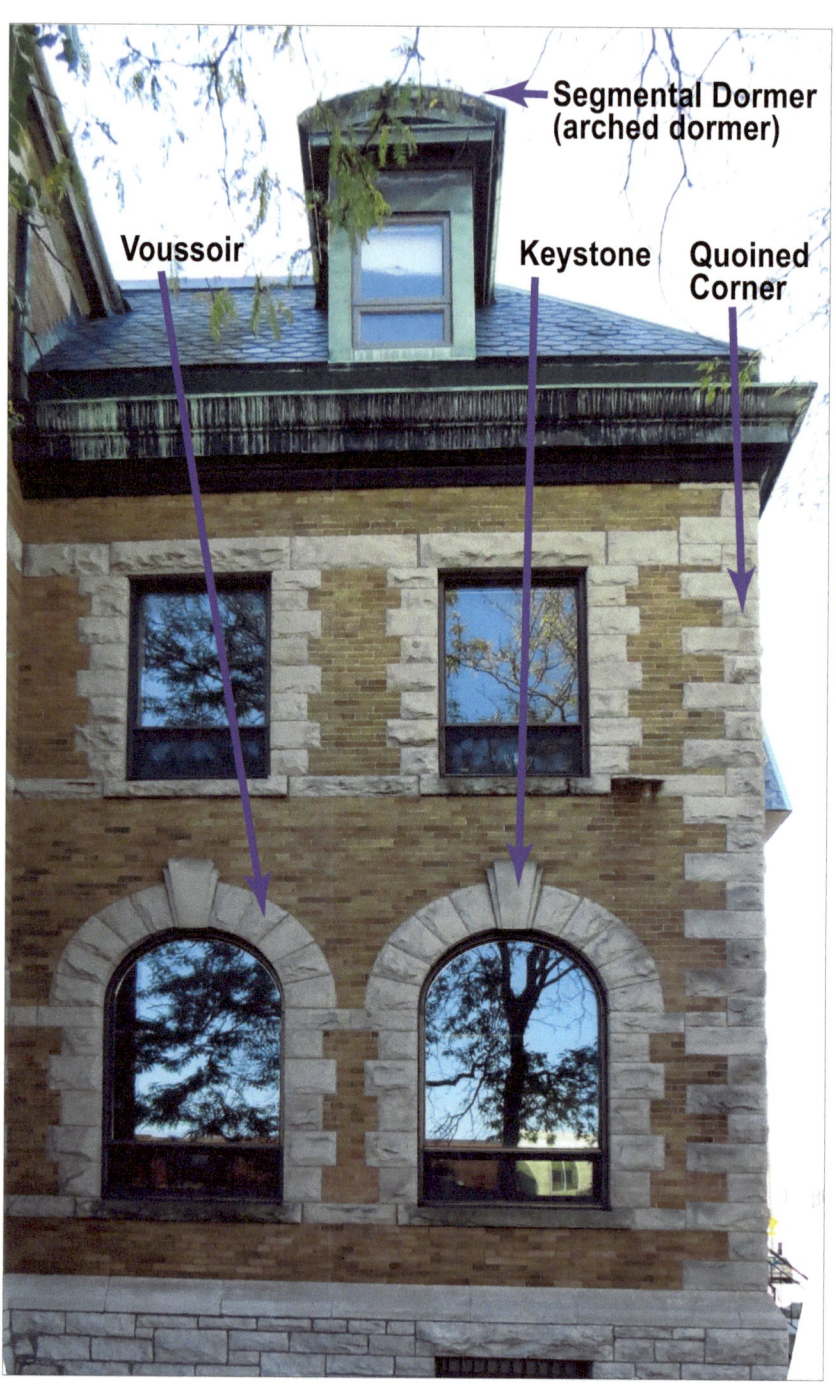

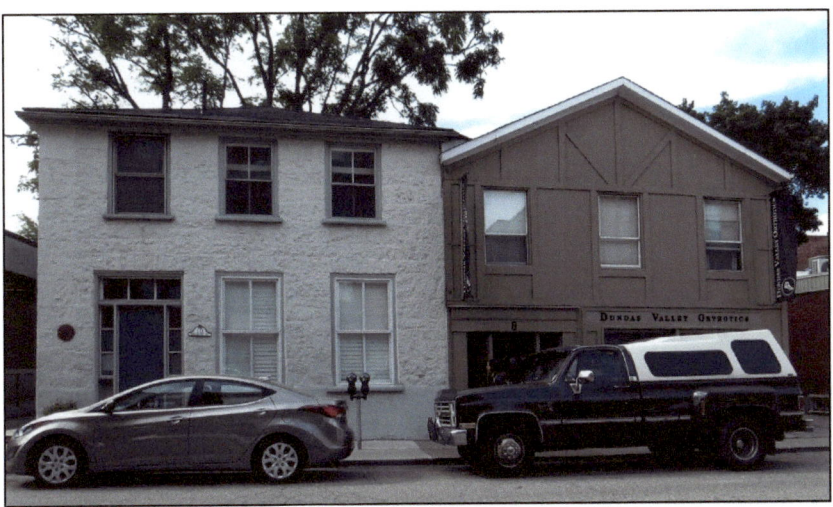

10 Ogilvie St. was built of rubble stone in 1835. The stone, in large blocks, is probably dolomite but is now heavily covered with white wash.

8 Ogilvie St. on the right has a Tudor influence and is home to Dundas Valley Orthotics.

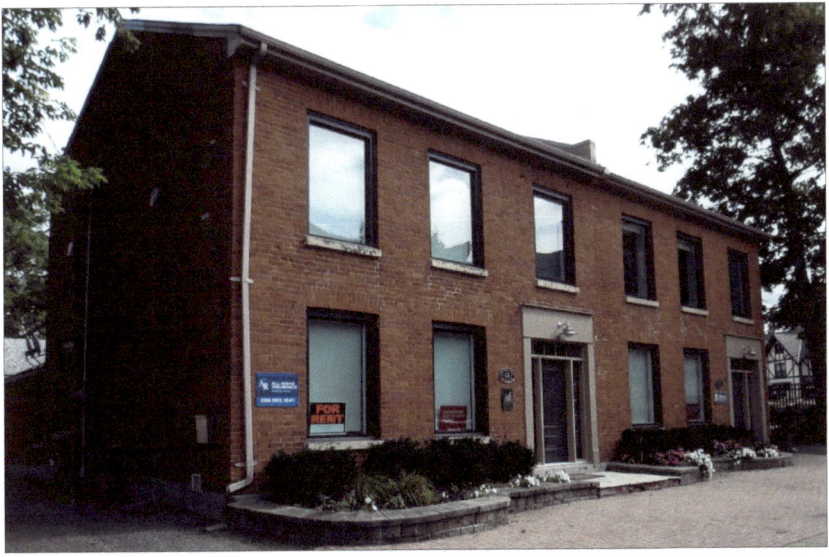

The Ware House at 15 Ogilvie St and The Wood House at 17 Ogilvie St. were built in 1850 before Canada was created.

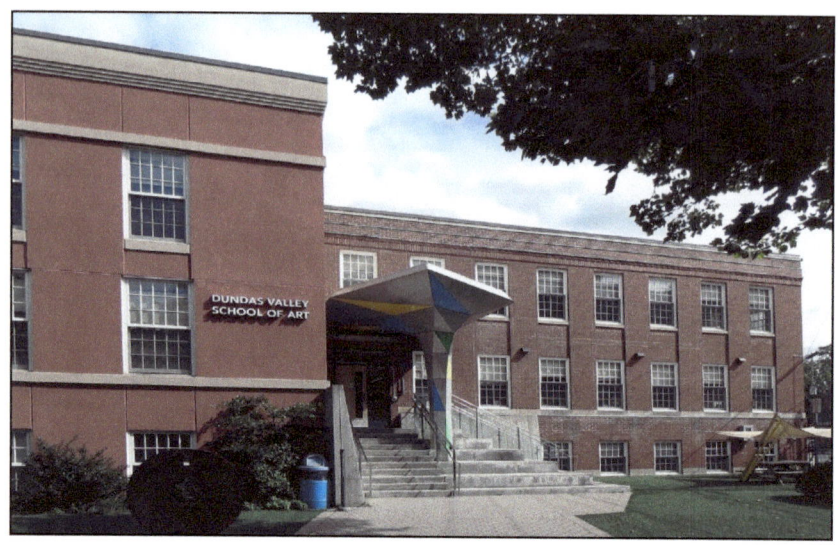

Built in the 1836, 21 Ogilvie Street is home to Dundas Valley School of Art. The building was the former home of a Wesleyan Ladies' College, Canada Screw Works, which later became Stelco, an aircraft engine plant, and a munitions factory during World War II. Munitions are weapons and ammunition, material, or equipment used in the war.

In 2010, Dundas Valley School of Art (DVSA) was able to secure Infrastructure Stimulus Funding, in partnership with the Carnegie Gallery and Dundas Museum & Archives.

DVSA's mission is to provide high quality, accessible, and 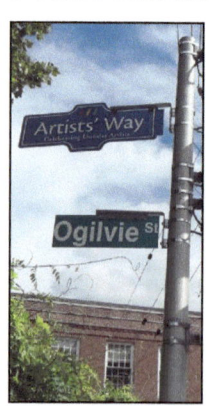 affordable visual arts education that encourages excellence and personal fulfillment for all ages. The DVSA was founded in 1964 by Marion Farnan and Emily Dutton, who recognized the need for professional-level art instruction in the region.

The Artists' Way sign was added to the traffic lights to celebrate Dundas artists.

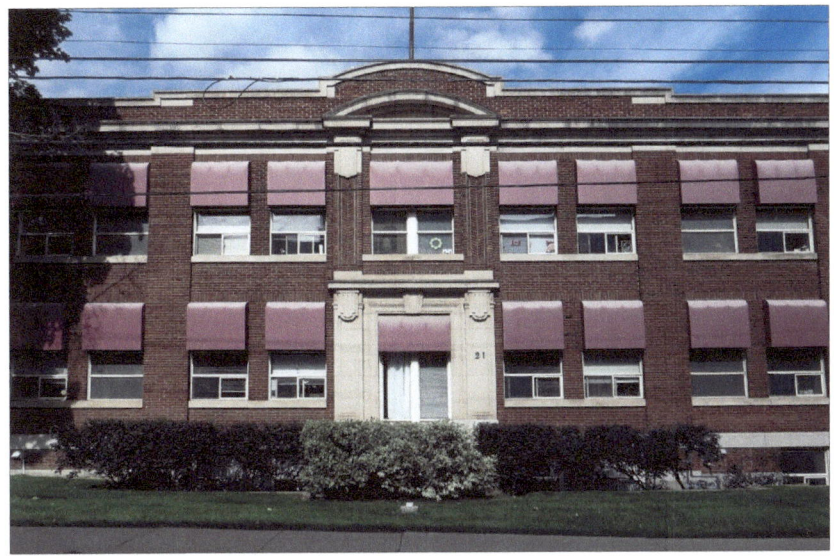

Bertram Place Retirement Living Centre is located at 21 Hatt St and Ogilvie. The photo on the left shows the original entrance that has been changed into a window.

The focal point has cast iron keystones and embellishments, pediment, and concrete windowsills.

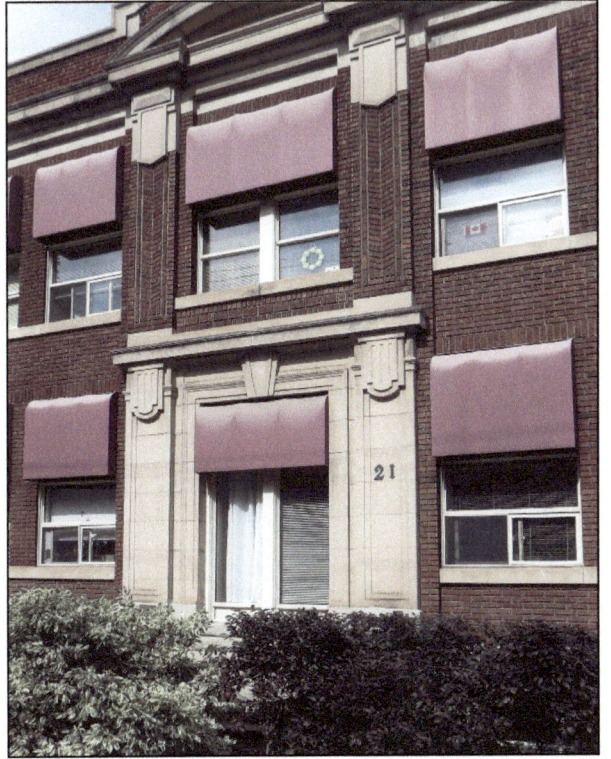

Barbara A. Fanson

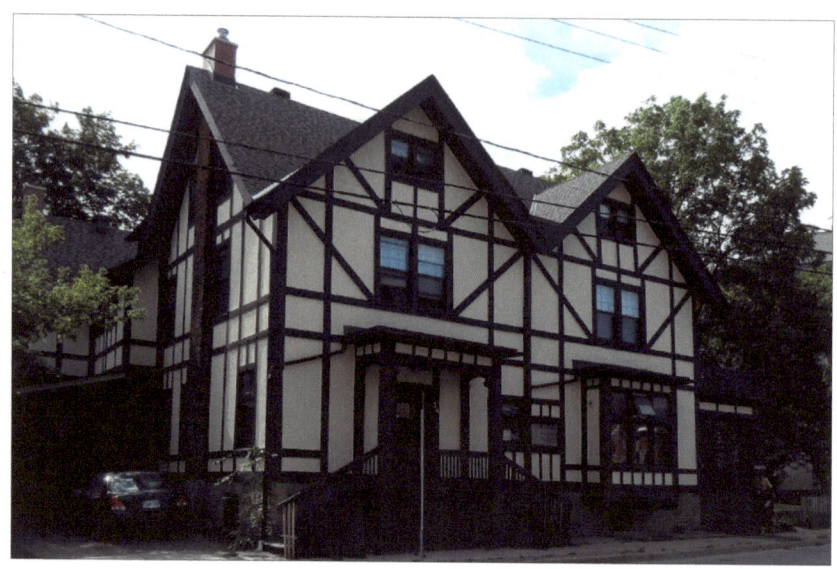

34 Hatt St. is a Tudor-style building with steeply pitched roof with side gables that "open" on the sides of the house and decorative (or false) half-timbering.

The Ellen Osler Memorial Home was founded in 1909 and was located at 34 Hatt Street, a building, which had been a private school. It was established by the Osler family, chiefly Sir Edmund Osler, in memory of Ellen Picton Osler (1806-1907), wife of Rev. Featherstone Lake Osler, who was Rector of St. James Church in Dundas from 1857 to 1879. She was the mother of Sir William Osler.

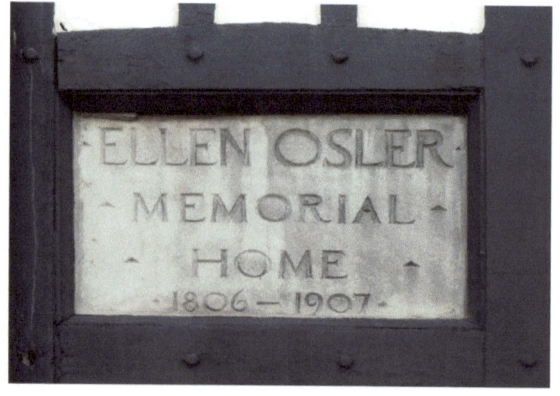

Ellen Osler is a Community Residential Facility funded through Correctional Services Canada and the Salvation Army.

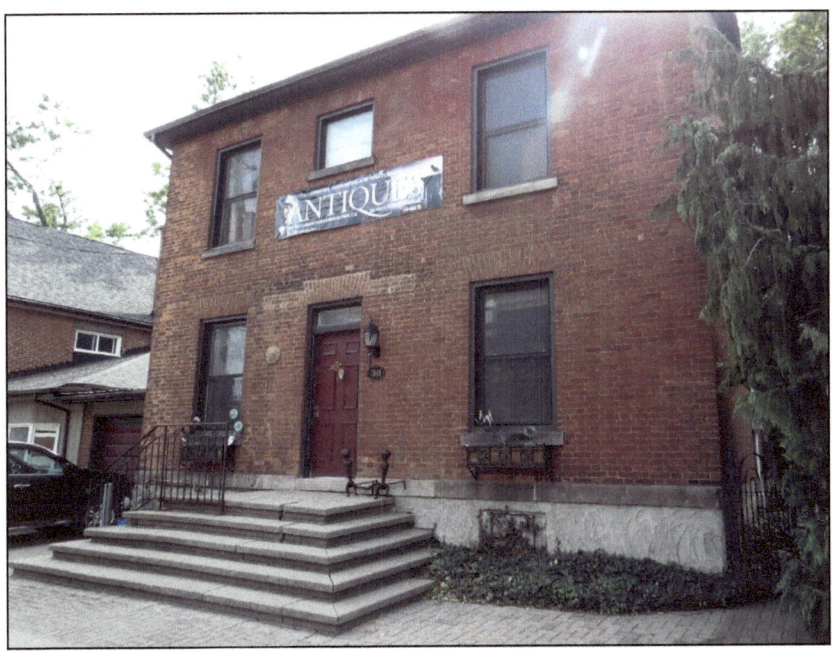

30 Hatt St. is a square building, typical of the Edwardian style. The front porch has been removed. Cabinet of Curiosities is an antique store.

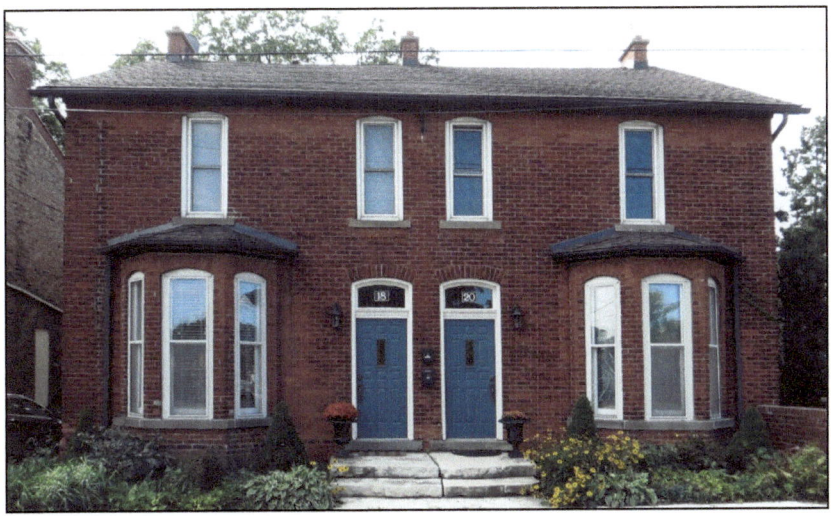

18 and 20 Hatt Street are symmetrical houses with an Edwardian style. They both have large bay windows and arched doors and windows.

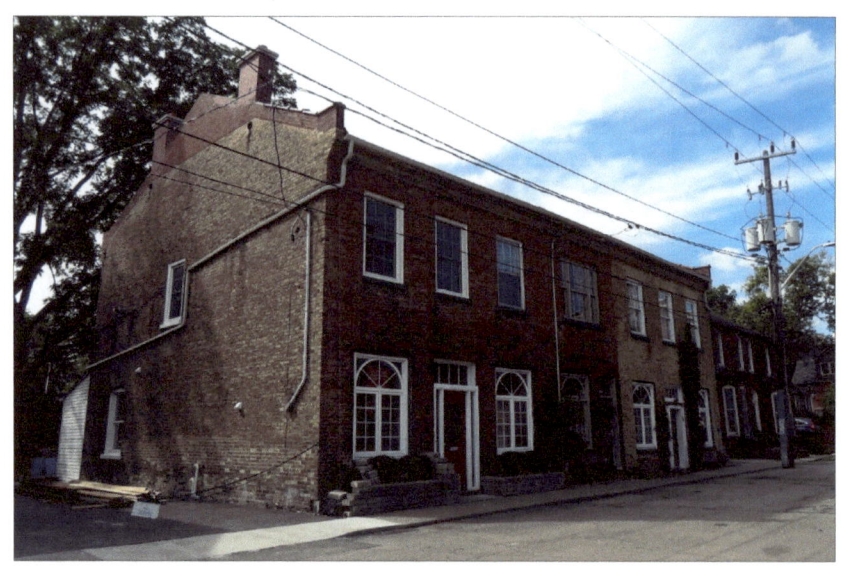

The row houses at 12, 14, and 16 Hatt Street have brackets under the roof.

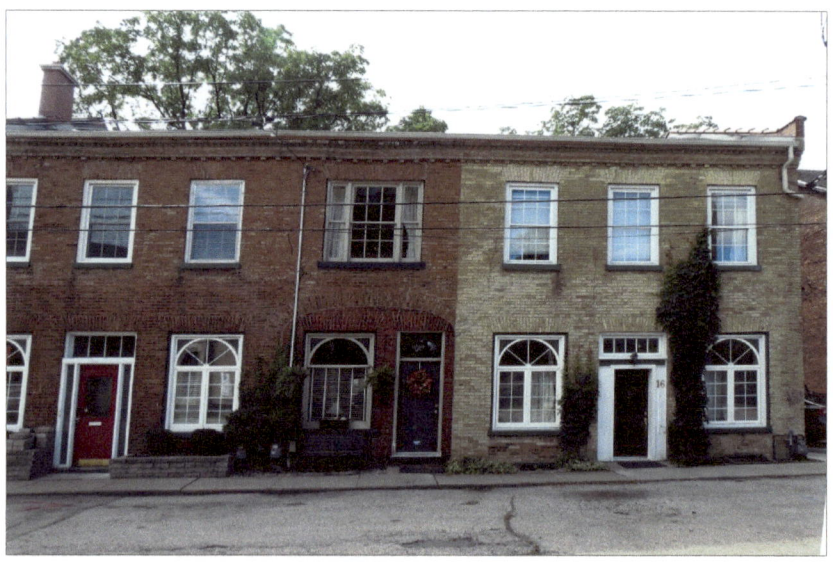

The row houses at 12, 14, and 16 Hatt Street.

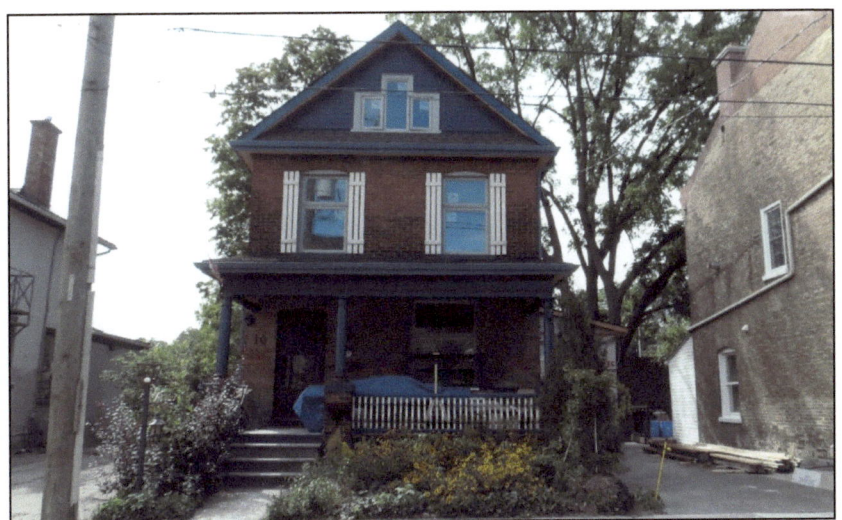

10 Hatt Street has a palladian window on the gable—3 windows with the middle one slightly bigger.
Edwardian architecture in the early 1900s was generally less ornate than Victorian architecture.

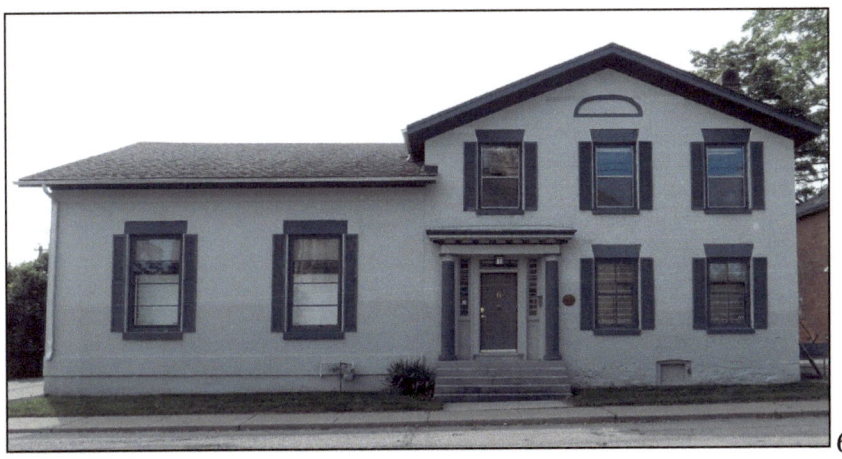

Hatt Street was built in the 1830s as a bank and then a police station in the 1980s, and then Alternative Audio. Now it is the office of Anderson Therapy Services, which has provided speech-language pathology, occupational therapy, instructor therapy, art therapy, and pediatric physiotherapy for over 23 years.

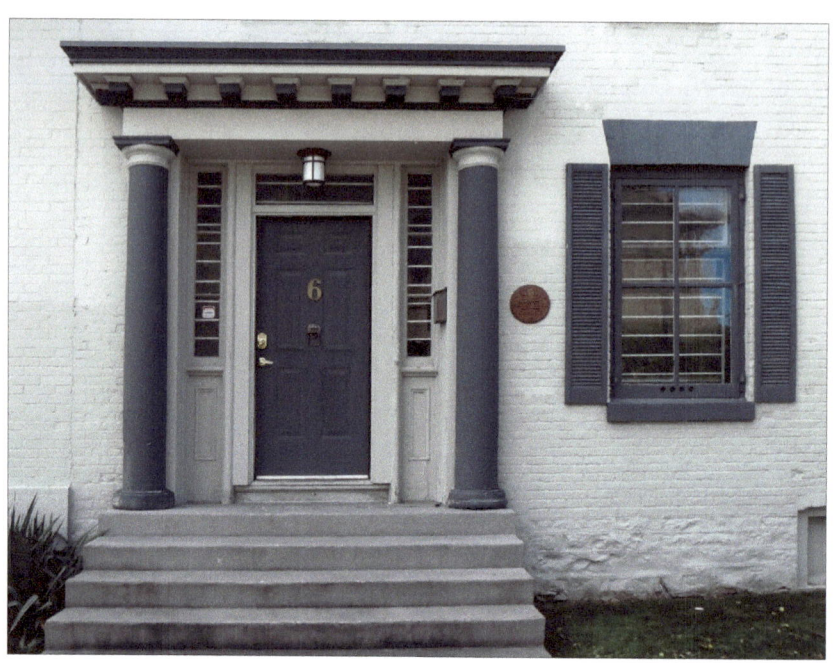

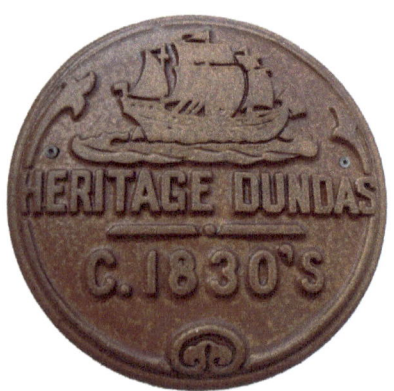

Notice the façade at the front of 6 Hatt Street. The Doric columns support the cornice with dentil blocks above the door. The Heritage Dundas plaque shows that the building was built in the 1830's.

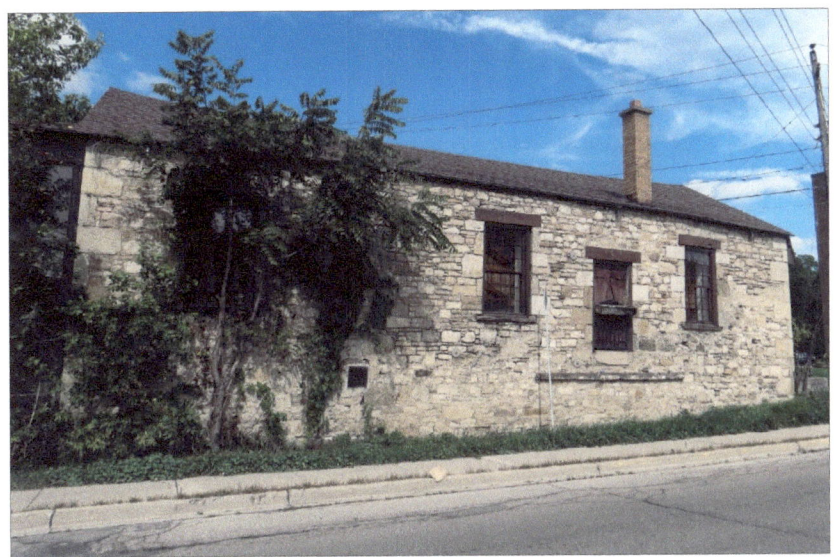

2 Hatt St. is the oldest building in Dundas. Built with local stone in 1804, it was Dundas' first post office, lighting store, an Art Gallery, and housed soldiers during the War of 1812.

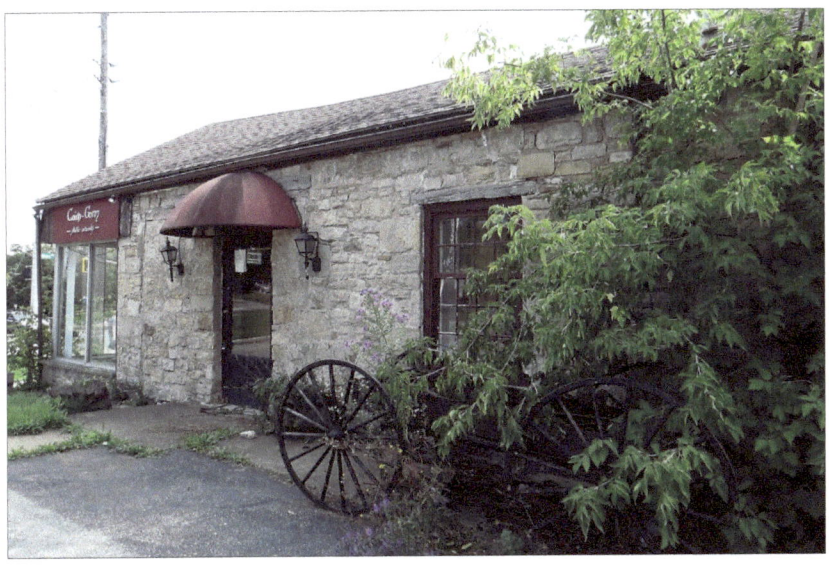

www.ingramcontent.com/pod-product-compliance
Lightning Source LLC
Chambersburg PA
CBHW040325220526
45473CB00009B/2573